Excellence in Giving Campaigns for 25 Years

HERB MILLER
WITH EUGENE GRIMM

CONSECRATION SUNDAY

Stewardship Program Guide
with Download Library

ABINGDON PRESS | NASHVILLE

**Consecration Sunday Stewardship Program Guide
with Download Library**

Copyright © 2007 by Herb Miller, Copyright © 2022 by Abingdon Press
All rights reserved.

No part of this work may be reproduced or transmitted in any form or by any means, electronic or mechanical, including photocopying and recording, or by any information storage or retrieval system, except as may be expressly permitted by the 1976 Copyright Act, the 1998 Digital Millennium Copyright Act, or in writing from the publisher. Requests for permission can be addressed to Rights and Permissions, The United Methodist Publishing House, 810 12th Avenue South, Nashville, TN 37203-4704 or e-mailed to permissions@abingdonpress.com.

978-1-791-02402-4

Unless otherwise noted, scripture quotations are from the New Revised Standard Version Bible, copyright © 1989 National Council of the Churches of Christ in the United States of America. Used by permission. All rights reserved worldwide. http://nrsvbibles.org/

Scripture quotations noted RSV are from Revised Standard Version of the Bible, copyright © 1946, 1952, and 1971 National Council of the Churches of Christ in the United States of America. Used by permission. All rights reserved worldwide. http://nrsvbibles.org/

Scripture quotations noted NEB are from the New English Bible, copyright © Cambridge University Press and Oxford University Press 1961, 1970. All rights reserved.

Scripture quotations noted JBP are from The New Testament in Modern English by J. B. Phillips copyright © 1960, 1972 J. B. Phillips. Administered by The Archbishops' Council of the Church of England. Used by Permission.

Scripture quotations noted ESV are from the ESV® Bible (The Holy Bible, English Standard Version®), copyright © 2001 by Crossway, a publishing ministry of Good News Publishers. Used by permission. All rights reserved.

22 23 24 25 26 27 28 29 30 31 — 10 9 8 7 6 5 4 3 2 1
MANUFACTURED IN THE UNITED STATES OF AMERICA

Contents

Instructions for Accessing the Download Library 4

Why *Consecration Sunday*? 5

The Big-Picture Overview of *Consecration Sunday* 9

Equipment for the Trip: *Consecration Sunday* 14

Selecting Your Guest Leader 15

Fielding Your Consecration Sunday Team 18

Detailed Road Map to *Consecration Sunday* 21

Tips for Announcements, Teaching, and Sermons.....................65

Beyond Second-Year Use of *Consecration Sunday* 73

Ten-year ABCs for Stewardship and Finance Committees..............77

Grow One Step Chart 90

Notes 92

Guest Leader Guide..97

Notes 109

Instructions for Accessing the Download Library

The *Consecration Sunday Stewardship Program Guide* includes a Download Library with letters, forms, and other useful communication tools to help your stewardship team implement the program. To access the Download Library, visit:

https://www.abingdonpress.com/consecrationsundayleader

Instructions for how and when to use each downloadable resource and how to adapt them for your congregation's needs are found in this *Program Guide*.

Why *Consecration Sunday*?

"Staying out of the red is a constant struggle in our church," said one of the pastors in a coffee-break conversation at a denominational cluster meeting. "So many board meetings turn negative when our resident financial pessimist quotes the bank balance and says, 'Can we really afford that?'"

"Balancing our budget has never been easier," said the pastor of a nearby church of about the same size. "We often discuss the right way to spend the money, but getting it is not the problem."

This conversation reflects two opposite financial conditions reported by thousands of congregations. What causes the sharp contrast? The cash-flow circumstances of "have" and "have-not" churches *correlate with the procedures by which they ask parishioners for contributions*.

Research has definitively answered the question, "What causes high per capita giving to congregations?" Churches across the United States ask people to contribute money in three different ways:

1. One kind of church takes *offerings*: They have no annual financial stewardship campaign. People in those congregations give an average of 1.5 percent of their income to support their church.
2. Researchers call the second kind of congregation a *pledging* church: The leaders build a proposed budget each year, then ask people to write on a pledge card the dollars per week or per month they plan to give and to turn in the card during an annual stewardship campaign. People in pledging congregations give an average of 2.9 percent of their income to their church. *In other words, people who write their financial commitments on paper give, on average, twice as much as people who do not write their intentions on paper.*

3. Researchers call the third kind of congregation a *percentage-giving* church. Instead of building a proposed budget, those churches conduct an annual stewardship campaign that asks people, "What percentage of your income do you feel God is calling you to give?" Parishioners then translate their answers into dollar amounts, write the figure on a card, and turn it in. The church creates the budget by totaling the cards. People in percentage-giving congregations contribute an average of 4.6 percent of their income to their church. *In other words, national research indicates that people whose churches repeatedly raise the question, "What percentage of your income is God calling you to give?" contribute three times more dollars per year than people whose churches only take offerings* (Dean R. Hoge, Charles Zech, Patrick McNamara, and Michael J. Donahue, *Money Matters* [Louisville: Westminster John Knox, 1996]).

This research also answers the question, "Why does the *Consecration Sunday Stewardship Program Guide* work so well?" Rather than requesting financial contributions to "pay the bills" or "support the budget," *Consecration Sunday* asks people to grow spiritually by giving a percentage of their income to the Lord's work through their congregations.

Perdue Research Group interviewed people in 150 congregations that have used *Consecration Sunday*. In 31 of those 150 churches, financial giving increased 25 percent or more the first year they used it. Another 37 of the 150 churches reported a 20 percent increase. Another 36 of the 150 churches experienced a 15 percent increase, and another 30 churches experienced a 10 percent increase. Only 16 of the 150 churches reported a 5 percent increase in giving. Of the 150 churches interviewed, 131 had used *Consecration Sunday* three or four years.

In one congregation, financial giving increased 25 percent the first year, 18 percent the second year, and 30 percent the third year. The congregation's financial secretary said, "Three reasons produced these annual increases. First, virtually no households lower their giving during the annual campaign. Second, between 66 percent and 88 percent of the households make some degree of annual increase. Third, four to six new households decided to tithe each year we used *Consecration Sunday*. These households, some of which grew from giving 4 percent of their income to giving 10 percent of their income, were a major part of our enormous annual increases."

This research also answers the question, "Why does spiritually focused stewardship education work better than fund-raising methods?" Over the past several decades, leaders in many churches have substituted secular fund-raising methods for Christian stewardship procedures. This happens because many board members of philanthropic community organizations also serve on their congregations' finance committees. Thus, when committee members decide how to ask their church's members to support its ministries, they often opt for the fund-raising procedures they have seen work in community organizations.

Fund-raising for nonprofit organizations in the community is as different from Christian stewardship as a bicycle is from an eighteen-wheeler. Both are valid forms of transportation, but they are not interchangeable. They accomplish two different goals. The goal of secular fund-raising is dollars for a worthy cause. The goal of Christian stewardship is the faithful management of all that God gives so that God can use our gifts to transform us spiritually and to extend Christ's transforming love to others. The apostle Paul spelled out those two goals in his lengthy definition of stewardship in 2 Corinthians 9:11-13.

Jesus summed up the spiritual connection between money and God this way: "Where your treasure is, there your heart will be also" (Luke 12:34). Financial stewardship is treasure management that helps us to escape the trap of selfishness by keeping ourselves spiritually focused on God.

Why *Consecration Sunday*? | **7**

Each of us makes one of two choices in life. We either become emotionally attached to our money, or we become emotionally attached to the God who gives us our money. Although we often hope to do both, in our hearts we know that cannot happen. Financial stewardship helps us to overcome the temptation to break the first commandment and put the false idol of money first, ahead of the God who revealed his love for us through Jesus Christ.

Yes, congregations that teach spiritually focused financial stewardship also occasionally use fund-raising methods. *Examples*: When the youth leaders collect money for a summer mission trip, when the women's organization holds a bake sale to support a worthy community cause, and when the church conducts a three-million-dollar capital campaign to build a family life center. All of these are fund-raising efforts whose objective is a specific amount of dollars to accomplish a specific ministry. However, those fund-raising endeavors are a tiny fraction of the annual giving in congregations that use spiritually focused stewardship education.

This research also answers the question, "Why are annual stewardship campaigns essential?" People do not drift into good giving habits. They decide into them. The reason they decide is because someone asks them to decide. An effective annual stewardship campaign is the best way to ask. In most congregations the illusion that high per capita giving can happen without some kind of annual campaign is just that: an illusion. Airplanes can fly all year, but they must land occasionally to take on fuel. Annual stewardship campaigns refuel church members' education regarding the spiritual connection between money and God.

Unfortunately, only four of ten Protestant congregations conduct any sort of annual stewardship campaign. This keeps many churches in the poverty-syndrome category (George Barna, *How to Increase Giving in Your Church* [Ventura, Calif.: Regal Books, 1997], pp. 99-100).

The Big-Picture Overview of *Consecration Sunday*

Looking at the broad outline of *Consecration Sunday*, we see seven major topographical features, supported by a Download Library (see the "Instructions for Accessing the Download Library" on page 4) that contains user-friendly resources to help you implement the program (for the how-to-do-it details, see subsequent sections of this book):

1. ***Consecration Sunday* assumes that laypeople do not like to visit other laypeople in their homes and ask them to fill out a pledge card.** Many laypeople refuse to do this. Even if they do it, many of them do it poorly. Therefore, *Consecration Sunday* asks attendees and members to complete an *Estimate of Giving Card* during morning worship on Consecration Sunday. At no point in the program do laypersons ask each other for money or pledges.
2. ***Consecration Sunday* teaches stewardship on the basis of the need of the giver to give for his or her own spiritual benefit rather than on the basis of the need of the church to receive to balance its budget.**
3. ***Consecration Sunday* focuses on the question, "What is God calling me to do?" rather than on the question, "What does the church need in order to pay its bills?"** Thus the annual stewardship emphasis becomes a spiritual-growth experience, not a fund-raising effort.
4. ***Consecration Sunday* focuses on tithing and percentage giving, not as a legalism, but as an appropriate faith commitment for which God's grace empowers us.** This does not mean that everyone in a congregation decides to tithe the first year of *Consecration Sunday*. But just because not everyone in a church is ready to give 10 percent of his or her income to the Lord's work, that does not mean we should avoid holding up tithing as a spiritual ideal.

5. **By asking people to complete *Estimate of Giving Cards* during a worship service, *Consecration Sunday* models the idea that stewardship is part of our worship of God, rather than a fund-raising procedure.**
6. ***Consecration Sunday* conducts the campaign before building the annual operating budget.** Setting the budget first, then raising the money, holds giving down. Church members, remembering the "fair share" motto of many secular organizations, make minor increases in their giving when they see that the new budget is only 4 percent higher than last year. Building the budget after the campaign takes the lid off potential increases by eliminating the fair-share, dues-paying syndrome and by eliminating the inevitable negative reaction everyone has to one or two items in the printed budget proposal.
7. ***Consecration Sunday* assumes that people can enjoy rather than feel negative about stewardship programs.**

Let's do a quick overview of how the Consecration Sunday Stewardship Program unfolds. This outline does not include the detailed how-to-do-it elements—found in subsequent sections of this book—but gives you a picture of how it works.

Step #1: *Your congregation selects as guest leader a pastor or layperson you are confident will follow the timeline instructions; can speak in an effective, interesting manner; and is available on the appropriate dates.* Guest leaders who meet those three criteria achieve the same results the first time they lead a *Consecration Sunday* as the tenth time they serve as a guest leader. *Consecration Sunday*'s results come from the process, not from the guest leader's personality. You might select as guest leader a judicatory staff person, a retired pastor who lives in your area, a pastor in a nearby community, or a capable layperson from another congregation. Sometimes, two pastors lead *Consecration Sunday* in each other's congregations (on consecutive Sundays, *not* on the same Sunday).

A guest leader is a necessity for several reasons. *(a)* People and pastor work harder. *(b)* The guest leader takes a fresh approach, which results in parishioners giving more attention and serious consideration to the subject. *(c)* Consecration Sunday team members are far less likely to take shortcuts. *(d)* Consecration Sunday teams make fewer mistakes since the pastor can suggest that "we telephone and check with the guest leader about that." *(e)* Since the presence of a guest leader makes a 10 to 30 percent difference in total financial results, he or she is well worth the small honorarium and travel expense.

Step #2: *The guest leader makes three trips to the church: (a)* About six to eight weeks prior to Consecration Sunday, the guest leader conducts a one-hour orientation session with the Consecration Sunday team that your church's governing board appoints to lead *Consecration Sunday*. Using detailed instructions in *Consecration Sunday* and the included "Guest Leader Guide" (see pages 97–108), he or she helps the Consecration Sunday team personalize the program for their congregation. *(b)* The guest leader speaks at the governing-board dinner on Sunday or Monday evening prior to Consecration Sunday. *(c)* The guest leader preaches during morning worship on Consecration Sunday.

Step #3: *Several kinds of publicity unfold during the four weeks before Consecration Sunday,* using several model letters and announcements.

Step #4: *On Sunday, two weeks before Consecration Sunday,* a Consecration Sunday team member requests Celebration Luncheon reservations from each person present. The majority of members make their reservations at that time. Large churches, in which this Celebration Luncheon is impractical, select from among the several other effective options a strategy that accomplishes the objectives of the Celebration Luncheon.

Step #5: *On Sunday morning, one week before Consecration Sunday,* another layperson repeats the request for Celebration Luncheon reservations during worship and the adult church school classes. Nobody asks anyone for money. Everything focuses on getting people to attend the worship service and Celebration Luncheon on Consecration Sunday.

Step #6: *On Sunday evening, one week before Consecration Sunday* (Monday evening in some communities), the guest leader speaks at a dinner for governing board members, committee chairpersons, ministry team chairpersons, church staff, Consecration Sunday team members, and the spouses of all these groups. No financial commitments are taken at this dinner; the presentation is inspirational and motivational stewardship education.

However, governing board members are requested to help contact all members and friends of the church who have not yet made their reservation for the Celebration Luncheon next Sunday. These contacts are made on the Monday, Tuesday, and Wednesday before Consecration Sunday. (This final week prior to Consecration Sunday is the only point at which large numbers of laypersons put time and energy into the program.)

Due to this systematic process, the attendance on Consecration Sunday is often 20 to 60 percent higher than usual. The whole church family shows up—the people who come every week, the people who come twice a month, the people who come once a month, and the people who come a couple of times a year.

Step #7: *On Consecration Sunday*, the guest leader preaches at morning worship and conducts a seven-minute commitment session at the end of the service, inviting people to fill out an *Estimate of Giving Card*.

When the guest leader invites members and friends to fill out their *Estimate of Giving Cards*, it is important to invite them to begin their new commitment period the week following Consecration Sunday or as soon thereafter as possible. If people put off beginning their new commitment until January (or the beginning of a fiscal year) a significant percentage of the increase will be lost.

Step #8: *The Celebration Luncheon on Consecration Sunday*, immediately following morning worship, is not a potluck. It is a catered meal that was not prepared by the people of the church. Some large churches with two, three, or four morning worship services successfully replace the Celebration Luncheon with a brunch after each service and a dessert fellowship for their

Saturday evening service. This accomplishes a key element of Consecration Sunday—namely, taking advance reservations. This ensures both a large attendance and large numbers of people focusing their attention on the question, "What percentage of my income is God calling me to give?"

Step #9: *The Celebration Luncheon involves no program except the announcement of the campaign results at the end of the meal.* The program preceded the luncheon; it was the worship service and the commitment session during worship. In most churches larger than 300 in average worship attendance, computing the results takes so much time that they usually announce the results in the newsletter and the Sunday morning worship bulletin the following week.

Step #10: *On Monday after Consecration Sunday*, the church office mails a letter that includes a stamped, self-addressed envelope and an *Estimate of Giving Card* to each household not present for Consecration Sunday.

Some people ask, "What is the best time of year to hold Consecration Sunday?" Many churches schedule Consecration Sunday in the fall between Labor Day and Thanksgiving. This fits perfectly if the congregation budgets on a calendar-year basis. It allows the budget to be created after completing the campaign so it can be put in force January 1.

Most congregations that budget on a July 1 fiscal-year basis schedule Consecration Sunday in the spring prior to Mother's Day. This gives them time to construct the budget and put it in force July 1.

People who have never experienced *Consecration Sunday*'s dramatic results often say it is hard for them to get used to this approach. It is so different from the way they have thought about stewardship in the past.

That is true. *Consecration Sunday* is different. That makes it a bit frightening for people who have never used it before. However, on the average, *Consecration Sunday* increases a church's financial contributions 15 to 30 percent per year. You will have no trouble whatever getting used to that.

Equipment for the Trip:
Consecration Sunday

To effectively execute the Consecration Sunday stewardship program, obtain the following from Cokesbury by calling 800-672-1789 or by visiting www.cokesbury.com:

- three copies of the *Consecration Sunday Stewardship Program Guide with Download Library* (one for the guest leader, one for the pastor, and one for the Consecration Sunday chairperson);
- seven *Consecration Sunday Team Member Manuals*; and
- sufficient *Estimate of Giving Cards* for your size church. Have these shipped to the guest leader and ask him or her to bring the cards on Consecration Sunday. This procedure prevents accidental distribution of the cards. Under no circumstances should you mail or distribute the *Estimate of Giving Cards* in advance of Consecration Sunday or prior to the end of the worship service that day.

To gain a clear understanding of the program, read the full *Consecration Sunday Stewardship Program Guide*. That prepares you to begin the journey toward an effective Consecration Sunday experience that helps attendees grow spiritually and adequately finances your congregation's mission and ministries.

Selecting Your Guest Leader

The guest leader you select visits the church three times.

First Trip: Six weeks or more prior to Consecration Sunday, the guest leader conducts a one-hour orientation meeting attended by the pastor, the Consecration Sunday chairperson, and the other seven members of the Consecration Sunday team.

Second Trip: The guest leader conducts a one-hour checkup meeting two hours prior to speaking at the governing board dinner one week before Consecration Sunday.

Third Trip: He or she preaches on Consecration Sunday morning and conducts the seven-minute commitment time, during which people complete *Estimate of Giving Cards* at the end of that service.

Selecting and scheduling the guest leader is totally in the local congregation's hands. The guest leader is not a professional fundraiser. The local congregation is totally in charge of setting honoraria and travel expenses for the guest leader, guided only by a sense of fairness, what is customary for guest speakers in that part of the country, and appropriate travel expenses for the three trips. (Note: Neither Abingdon Press nor Eugene Grimm receives any portion of the honoraria that congregations pay guest leaders.)

Select a pastor or lay leader in your area in whom you have confidence. Experiences in thousands of congregations indicate that someone who has never led a Consecration Sunday Stewardship Program—provided that person has good public-speaking ability and carefully studies and meticulously follows the *Consecration Sunday "Guest Leader Guide"* (pages 97–108)—is as effective the first time as the tenth time.

If you do not know an experienced guest leader, select someone you respect as a speaker. *Possibilities*: A regional denominational staff member, such as a district superintendent. A retired pastor often fills this role effectively. *Warning: He or she must not be a member of your congregation!* In some settings two pastors can lead *Consecration Sunday* in each other's congregations. (In such instances, however, do not schedule Consecration Sundays on the same day! Each pastor should be present in his or her own church on its Consecration Sunday.)

Note: Neither Abingdon Press nor Eugene Grimm maintains lists of guest leaders. Often, however, someone in your regional denominational office is aware of possible guest leaders in your area. If not, contact the regional offices of other denominations for the names of possible guest leaders. *Consecration Sunday* is used in the congregations of more than 25 denominations. Examples include The United Methodist Church, Presbyterian Church (U.S.A.), Episcopal Church, Evangelical Lutheran Church in America, Missouri Synod Lutheran Church, North American Lutheran Church, United Church of Christ, American Baptist Church, and Christian Church (Disciples of Christ).

The guest leader, pastor, Consecration Sunday chairperson, and the other seven team members study the detailed instructions in *Consecration Sunday*, including the "Guest Leader Guide," and the *Team Member Manual*. What should you do in the extremely unlikely event that you ask the guest leader a question to which he or she cannot find an answer in this book? Ask your guest leader to email eugenegrimm@me.com with the question. Please place "Consecration Sunday question" in the subject line. (Due to Eugene Grimm's schedule, allow 48 hours for a response.)

Warning: Avoid making the guest leader into a "guest speaker" by leaving him or her out of the leadership function! For maximum results, he or she visits the congregation on the three important occasions detailed in this book and provides active leadership. Do not short-circuit your financial results by merely employing him or her as a "guest speaker."

Note: Stewardship preaching resources are listed on pages 70–72. Experience in countless churches has proven the value and necessity of a guest leader. Trying to save money by doing

Consecration Sunday without a guest leader is an expensive mistake. Even if your pastor has served as a guest leader in other congregations, a guest leader for your congregation generates ten to twenty times more money than his or her honorarium and travel expense. Why?

- **Someone other than your pastor takes a fresh approach to stewardship.** Thus, parishioners give the subject greater attention and think about their giving in new ways.
- **The Consecration Sunday team and the pastor work more diligently and carefully.** Team members are far less likely to take shortcuts that reduce final results.
- **In case local leaders insist on cutting out some of the steps, your pastor can say, "Let's telephone and check with the guest leader before we make a change in the program."**
- **The mistake of not having a guest leader compounds in subsequent years.** Having done the program wrong the first time, the congregation usually repeats its mistake. This escalates a costly mistake to astronomical financial heights, blocking many members from the spiritual-growth benefits that would have come from their decisions to move toward percentage-giving habits.

Secure a guest leader. Provide him or her with a copy of the *Consecration Sunday Stewardship Program Guide*. Order from Cokesbury and have shipped to your guest leader, the complete bulk of sufficient *Estimate of Giving Cards* for a congregation of your size. Insist that he or she not deviate from the instructions. *Consecration Sunday* was rewritten seventy times during its extensive field-testing several years ago—and rewritten again in two previous versions. *Consecration Sunday* addresses feedback observations from hundreds of pastors and guest leaders. It works if everyone follows its instructions.

Fielding Your Consecration Sunday Team

When should the guest leader hold the orientation meeting with the Consecration Sunday team? Six to eight weeks before Consecration Sunday works best. Four weeks ahead of Consecration Sunday is the absolute minimum. Fewer weeks than that leave too little time to properly execute the Consecration Sunday Stewardship Program.

Prior to your guest leader orientation meeting, select your Consecration Sunday chairperson and the other seven team members. Make sure they can be present (but do not ask them to do a particular task at the time you recruit them). Also, be certain that the pastor is available to sit in on this meeting. Even if the pastor has been involved in previous Consecration Sundays in the congregation, it is important that she or he be aware of the progression and who will be serving as team speaker for each week. At the one-hour orientation, the guest leader hands each team member a copy of the *Team Member Manual*, walks through the timeline in detail, asks team members to fill in the dates on their copy of the *Team Member Manual*, leads the group in deciding which persons are to handle specific responsibilities, and leads them in writing appropriate team member names in the blanks provided for that purpose. When team members leave the meeting, each person knows exactly what to do and when, because each person now has a *Team Member Manual* in which he or she has written the various dates leading up to Consecration Sunday, along with his or her responsibilities.

How do you pick the Consecration Sunday chairperson and the other seven team members? Some of them could be members of your congregation's stewardship or finance committee. However, the best teams are usually a special task force formed for this purpose and year.

Responsibility List and Names of Our Consecration Sunday Team Members

1. _____ Consecration Sunday Chairperson

2. _____ Celebration Luncheon Chairperson

3. _____ Congregational Governing Board Dinner Telephone Chairperson

4. _____ Announcer #1 makes morning worship and Sunday school announcements three weeks before Consecration Sunday by following the printed instructions for this announcement in the "Detailed Road Map to *Consecration Sunday*" on pages 21–64.

5. _____ Announcer #2 presents the "Grow One Step" sheet during morning worship two weeks before Consecration Sunday. This person's announcement is longer and more complex than that of the other two announcers. He or she should be articulate, comfortable with public speaking, and follow with precision the printed instructions for this announcement in the "Detailed Road Map to *Consecration Sunday*" on pages 21–64.

6. _____ Announcer #3 makes morning worship and Sunday school announcements one week before Consecration Sunday by following the printed instructions for this announcement in the "Detailed Road Map to *Consecration Sunday*" on pages 21–64.

Fielding Your Consecration Sunday Team

7. _____ Church Financial Secretary makes advance computations in preparation for speedy final calculations right after worship on Consecration Sunday. Variations of this procedure: Churches with fewer than 300 in average worship attendance usually announce the total results by the time people finish eating the Celebration Luncheon on Consecration Sunday. To accomplish this calculation rapidly, the financial secretary should recruit an assistant for Consecration Sunday morning. In most churches with an average worship attendance of more than 300, the financial secretary completes the calculations during the week following Consecration Sunday. The results are announced during worship the following Sunday morning and are published in the church newsletter the following week.

8. _____ Congregational Prayer Chair enlists a team to pray daily for the success of the Consecration Sunday Stewardship Program. Several items should be included in their daily prayers:

   A. Pray for the Consecration Sunday team members as they lead the program.
   B. Pray that their congregation will, more than ever, be a house of prayer.
   C. Pray that all members of the congregation will seek God's will for them and for their families in coming to a faithful decision regarding what God is calling each to give.
   D. Pray for the guest leader as she or he leads the program and that God will grant him or her the words to say to encourage a faithful response to God's call.

Detailed Road Map to *Consecration Sunday*

At your Consecration Sunday team's orientation meeting six to eight weeks before Consecration Sunday, your guest leader guides the team in writing the appropriate dates for your congregation in the blanks. The orientation session moves faster when your guest leader, pastor, and Consecration Sunday chairperson have agreed on the Consecration Sunday date and the guest leader has had time to complete his or her timeline prior to the session.

Warning: Study the instruction steps carefully and accomplish its details to the letter. Everything you change reduces the end result (total number of dollars given by your people). Avoid using the program's name, *Consecration Sunday*, without actually doing the program. The results come from following the program's instructions, NOT from using the name.

Warning: Remind the team that Jesus never apologized for talking about money. Can you imagine Jesus beginning to talk about money with the phrase, "I'm sorry to talk about money, but…".

To ensure clarity, the timeline states methods that work and several ways that do not work. To increase user-friendliness, all of the model letters and printed communication aids for accomplishing *Consecration Sunday* are integrated into this timeline. You can also download them from the Download Library that accompanies this book (see the "Instructions for Accessing the Download Library" on page 4). Also sprinkled through the timeline are questions many church leaders ask about timeline items, plus answers based on the experiences of thousands of congregations.

Question: May we photocopy parts of the *Stewardship Program Guide* or the "Guest Leader Guide"?

Answer: Only those pages where explicit photocopy permission is printed, and then only for congregations that purchase and use the material locally.

United States and international copyright laws protect all other parts of the *Consecration Sunday Stewardship Program Guide* and "Guest Leader Guide," its accompanying Download Library, the *Consecration Sunday Team Member Manual*, and the *Estimate of Giving Card*.

Question: **Why not print a one-page timeline of dates and tasks to distribute among the team members?**

Answer: Don't do it! That list is already in the book and a one-page list is intentionally not included. Field testing indicates that *(a)* the book's layout, asking people to write in the blanks the dates and names of people who will assume various responsibilities—interspersed with often-asked Questions and Answers—gets excellent results; *(b)* this layout provides an educational process by which each team member learns *what to do*, and *what not to do*, and *why*; *(c)* team members learning what does NOT work is as important as knowing the list of dates and tasks, and the book's layout accomplishes that objective—whereas handing out a short list of dates and tasks can prevent the achievement of that objective; *(d)* when the team members work together as a group to understand their roles, a positive group process happens—which cannot happen when someone merely hands the team members a list of dates and tasks, and *(e)* the objective of Consecration Sunday is NOT merely to do a program but to educate people regarding what works and does not work to increase financial stewardship in congregations.

_____ **(Write in your local date and time.) Six or more weeks prior to Consecration Sunday:** The guest leader holds a one-hour orientation session with the Consecration Sunday team. *Warning: Do not attempt to do this program without a guest leader. The results decrease drastically.* The guest leader visits the church three times, once for this orientation session, once for a Consecration Sunday team checkup meeting two hours prior to speaking at the governing board dinner one week before Consecration Sunday, and once to preach during morning worship on Consecration Sunday. Eliminating one or more of those visits appreciably reduces Consecration Sunday's financial results.

Question: **Must the guest leader be present for all three events—the orientation session, the governing board dinner, and morning worship on Consecration Sunday?**

Answer: Three trips obtain the best end results. Each absence diminishes your financial and spiritual growth outcome. However, if he or she absolutely cannot make one of the three trips, missing the orientation session does the least damage. His or her presence at the governing board dinner one week prior to Consecration Sunday and at the Consecration Sunday worship service is essential to positive financial results.

Question: **What if we have never asked people to complete *Estimate of Giving Cards* before and a few of our lay leaders resist this concept?**

Answer: On average, people who write their financial stewardship intentions on a card during annual campaigns give two or three times as much per year as people who refuse to fill out such cards. Very few people respond negatively to this kind of biblically based, spiritually focused campaign.

The program in no way publicly embarrasses people who prefer not to complete a card. During the commitment session at the end of worship on Consecration Sunday, the guest leader says something like the following: "This is an opportunity for us to make a commitment to God's ministries in and through our congregation. However, there may be people here who for conscientious reasons prefer not to make this kind of commitment. If that is your preference, we want you to feel comfortable in not participating."

In every church a few people do not complete an *Estimate of Giving Card*, but that percentage is always small. The number will grow smaller each year your church uses *Consecration Sunday*.

In one church the financial secretary said after three years, "This thing amazes me. Three years ago, old Joe said, 'I'm never going to fill out one of those cards!' You know what? Today when I tallied the cards, Joe's card was there."

One of the reasons Joe changed his mind is because nobody told him he had to. Never assume that people have permanently made up their minds about anything. People can grow. They can change. They can reassess things and move in new directions. The more freedom you give them to decide for themselves, the more likely they are to change.

Question: **What about people who say, "My giving is personal, between me and God, so I don't want to sign a card"?**

Answer: This is a mythical belief. In virtually every case where people regularly contribute more than loose change or dollar bills to their church, *someone other than God knows*. The financial secretary who records and deposits the money knows. Exceptions to this rule never exceed 1 percent of a congregation's members, since virtually everyone wants to take advantage of the income tax break for charitable donations.

Question: **Couldn't we get the total anticipated income by just asking people to fill out the *Estimate of Giving Cards* anonymously, without signing them?**

Answer: Research across the country indicates that people who complete cards without signing them—often called the "Faith Promise" procedure—give an average of 30 percent less per year than people who sign the cards. If your church leaders put out the effort to conduct a Consecration Sunday Stewardship Program, why compromise the outcome by adding a procedure known to reap smaller results?

Question: **Why have a prayer team? Couldn't we just invite members to pray during the team member talks?**

Answer: By all means, each person giving a stewardship talk in the weeks running up to Consecration Sunday should invite people to pray. However, in stewardship programs where there is a specific prayer leader and team, *(a)* people tend to take it more seriously, and *(b)* the focus on prayer helps members grasp the overarching theme that Consecration Sunday is about spiritual growth rather than just raising more dollars.

Monday, _____ (write your local date in this and each successive blank), four weeks before Consecration Sunday: Create numerous posters to hang around the church that say, "It's Coming _____ (date)."
Warning: Make these posters yourself. Do NOT add additional words or information to the posters!

Monday, _____ (four weeks prior to Consecration Sunday): Prepare for this week's church newsletter the article (shown on page 26, available in the Download Library), signed by the governing board chairperson, and post the same article to your church's website in the section for news and announcements, or on your pastor's or staff blog. (With the term "governing board" as with other applicable instances, change the wording to match your congregation's customary terminology.)

Download the *Church Newsletter Article* **(shown on page 26) from the Download Library for the initial announcement of Consecration Sunday in your church.** *Note:* **Copyright permission is granted to use only in your congregation.** *Warning:* **Do not change words, add sentences, or delete sentences! Alterations risk damaging final results (significant increases in financial giving and the spiritual growth of donors).**

Download the *It's Coming* **meme (shown on page 27) from the Download Library and share via your church's social media channels along with the following text: "It's coming _____ [date of your church's Consecration Sunday]." Include a link to the Church Newsletter Article on the website or blog.**

(Dated four weeks before Consecration Sunday)

Consecration Sunday Is Coming

Congregations that approach financial stewardship from a biblical perspective do not view the money Christians give to their church merely as a way to pay its bills. Rather, such congregations see financial contributions as a way to help people grow spiritually in their relationship with God by supporting their church's mission and ministry with a percentage of their incomes.

Our congregation's finance committee has selected the *Consecration Sunday Stewardship Program* as a way to teach the biblical and spiritual principles of generous giving in our stewardship education emphasis this year.

Consecration Sunday is based on the biblical philosophy of the need of the giver to give for his or her own spiritual development, rather than on the need of the church to receive. Instead of treating people like members of a social club who should pay dues, we will treat people like followers of Jesus Christ who want to give unselfishly as an act of discipleship. *Consecration Sunday* encourages people toward proportionate and systematic giving in response to the question, "What percentage of my income is God calling me to give?"

During morning worship on Consecration Sunday, we are asking our attendees and members to make their financial commitments to our church's missionary, benevolent, and educational ministries in this community and around the world.

Every attendee and member who completes an *Estimate of Giving Card* does so voluntarily by attending morning worship on Consecration Sunday. We urge people to attend who feel strongly opposed to completing a card. The procedure is done in such a way that no one feels personal embarrassment if he or she chooses not to fill out a card.

We will do no home solicitation to ask people to complete cards. During morning worship our guest leader will conduct a brief period of instruction and inspiration, climaxed by members making their commitments as a confidential act of worship.

We will encourage participation in Consecration Sunday events through the Consecration Sunday team and governing board members. Since we will make no follow-up visits to ask people to complete their cards, we will make every effort to inform, inspire, and commit everyone to attend Consecration Sunday worship.

Thanks in advance for your enthusiastic participation in Consecration Sunday events.

Governing Board Chairperson,

IT'S COMING MEME

CONSECRATION SUNDAY

IT'S COMING

Sunday, _____ (three weeks before Consecration Sunday): The Consecration Sunday team's Announcer #1 makes a brief announcement in adult church school classes and morning worship regarding the importance of Consecration Sunday and the Celebration Luncheon on _____, _____ (day and date). Do *not* stress the church's need for funds! Do *not* try to shame or guilt-trip people into generosity! Those approaches create negative results: anger and resentment toward the church and the announcer! Stress each giver's need to grow spiritually by contributing a specific percentage of his or her income as a commitment to Jesus Christ. Remind people that the Celebration Luncheon is not a potluck dinner but a catered meal for which they make reservations. As part of his or her morning worship announcement, announcer #1 includes a brief personal witness to his or her convictions regarding the value of financial stewardship. For ideas, see the section of this book titled "Tips for Announcements, Teaching, and Sermons" (pages 65–72). If, in addition to adult church school classes, your congregation has several small groups that meet during the week, make provisions to include those groups in the three weeks of announcements. At the conclusion of the talk, be sure to invite everyone to join the prayer team in praying for:

- the success of the Consecration Sunday Stewardship Program,
- that members may grow spiritually as they grow in their giving, and
- that the leadership team and the congregation will find that in addition to spiritual growth, they find stewardship fun.

Download the *What Percentage* meme from the Download Library and share via your church's social media channels.

WHAT PERCENTAGE MEME

CONSECRATION SUNDAY

WHAT PERCENTAGE OF MY INCOME IS GOD CALLING ME TO GIVE?

Monday, _____ (three weeks before Consecration Sunday): Mail letter #1 (shown on page 30) to all members and regular attendees; in other words, everyone who actively participates in your congregation. Stick with the letter's basic outline. Change only the information needed to personalize it for your congregation. *Change example*: A large church with multiple services may decide to modify the Celebration Luncheon's procedures based on the options listed on page 31. Share the Celebration Luncheon Invitation meme (shown on page 29) via your church's social media channels.

While mailed letters have often received the best results in the past, we are aware that email has become a way of life today for nearly everyone. It is a fact that in the busy-ness of our present lifestyles, letters can unfortunately be laid aside and without some special reminder, emails may be placed on the back-burner. If your church chooses to use an email approach due to the cost of mailed letters or lack of personnel to mail them, please include a note in the subject line like, "Important email from your church: PLEASE open and read immediately."

Download the *Celebration Luncheon Invitation* meme from the Download Library. Share via your church's social media channels along with the following text: "Sunday, _____ [date] is our congregation's Consecration Sunday. Join us for worship and the Celebration Luncheon."

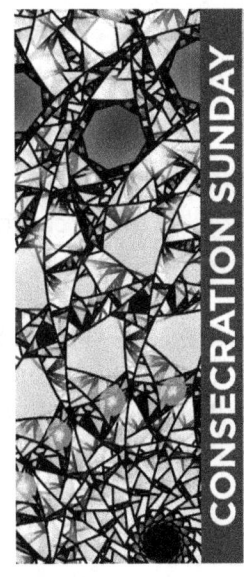

Download Letter #1 (shown on page 30) from the Download Library. Personalize the dates and church name. Print on church stationery. *Note*: Copyright permission is granted to use only in your congregation. *Warning*: Do not change words, add sentences, or delete sentences! Alterations risk damaging final results (significant increases in financial giving and the spiritual growth of donors).

LETTER #1

_____ [Dated Monday, three weeks before Consecration Sunday]

Dear Members and Friends of _____ Church:

Sunday, _____, is our congregation's Consecration Sunday. I urge you to plan now to attend the two important events: Sunday morning worship and the Celebration Luncheon immediately following worship that same day (a catered meal, not a potluck dinner).

This spiritual-growth-oriented process is designed to enrich our biblical understanding of Christian stewardship. Rather than focusing on the need of the church to receive, the experience concentrates on the need of the giver to give for his or her own spiritual development.

We believe that you are concerned enough to attend on Consecration Sunday and make your financial commitment as an act of worship in the church sanctuary.

No one will call on you at your home for a pledge. But we will contact you personally to secure your commitment to attend morning worship on Consecration Sunday and the Celebration Luncheon immediately after worship.

Cordially,

Governing Board Chairperson

Question: **How do we handle the Celebration Luncheon on Consecration Sunday if we have more than one worship service?**

Answer: The Consecration Sunday team should adopt one of the following options during the guest leader orientation session.

- If your church is in a small town, you have two morning worship services, and attendance at the early service is sparse, most first-service attendees will return for a noon meal.
- If your church is in a metropolitan area where many first-service attendees drive a great distance, schedule a brunch after the first service and a luncheon after the second service.
- If you have two, three, or four morning worship services, schedule a brunch after each service.
- One Roman Catholic church scheduled and took reservations for six dessert fellowships following six masses from Saturday through Sunday evening.

If you elect to schedule two or more brunches, either *(a)* tabulate and report the financial commitments from each service at each brunch, *(b)* report the results during morning worship the next Sunday, or *(c)* report the results in the next week's church newsletter and morning worship bulletin.

Question: **Are you sure the catered meal is necessary?**

Answer: The Celebration Luncheon meal is a *crucial* element in obtaining *Consecration Sunday* results! The reservations for the dinner get a large number of bodies to the building—a major percentage more of the congregation than will come without the dinner reservations. If the bodies are at the building, the minds consider stewardship commitments in a way that never happens when the bodies are NOT at the building.

Nothing in this program is theoretical; we are talking here about what works! Field-testing in hundreds of congregations in 25 denominations during the last several years reveals that deleting that catered meal drastically reduces the results (amount of increases in giving and the spiritual growth of donors). Without the luncheon, you are NOT doing *Consecration Sunday*: you are talking about a very different program of your own devising.

The meal must not be a standard fellowship dinner to which everyone brings food, because that eliminates the need to secure reservations for the meal. Removing the reservation procedure can drastically reduce the sizable crowd that always results from this procedure, thus eliminating a great part of the positive financial results. However, the quality of the meal is not the central issue! The meal can be inexpensive to prepare. The meal can be served cafeteria-line style, if that is the most convenient procedure in your facilities. See other options below.

When your church's financial support increases 15 percent or 20 percent or 30 percent by using *Consecration Sunday*, how expensive is the Celebration Luncheon? Most people consider as good stewardship an investment of God's money that brings such significant returns.

Successful ways to accomplish the Celebration Luncheon's catered meal—in contrast to contracting with a professional caterer—have included the following:

- In one church, a member who is a professional caterer prepared the meal at a reduced price.
- In another church, the women's organization from a neighboring congregation prepared the meal at a reduced price.
- In another congregation, the man responsible for the annual community barbecue took charge of preparing the meal, got a rancher to donate a steer, and catered a barbecue luncheon at a reduced cost.
- In another church, the congregation's governing board members decided to donate the cost of and to prepare the Celebration Luncheon.
- In another church, two affluent governing board members believed in Consecration Sunday so strongly that they volunteered to cover the

Celebration Luncheon cost the first year their congregation used it. The financial results were so substantial that no one argued against the church budget covering the luncheon in subsequent years.

Do not under any circumstances ask for donations at the Celebration Luncheon! Both this year and in subsequent years, asking for donations decreases attendance and causes people to feel that they need not make a reservation; thus, reducing the attendance and the financial results of *Consecration Sunday*.

By contrast, however, you can allow people to pay for their meals at the dinner for governing board, committee chairpersons, and Consecration Sunday team members on the Sunday or Monday evening prior to Consecration Sunday.

Despite its essential value, experiences in thousands of congregations across the United States indicate that local leaders are tempted to try to save money by leaving out the catered Celebration Luncheon on Consecration Sunday. This shortcut is a short circuit. Do not fall prey to the illusion that your church is an exception to this "must do it" rule. Such judgment calls by local leaders are like standing on an airport runway and saying, "I am an exception to the law of gravity. I can fly without the aid of an airplane."

Question: **What if lack of meal space is the major issue?**

Answer: Use ingenuity to figure out how to address the space challenge so that you can take reservations for either a noon luncheon, brunches after each service, and/or a dessert fellowship if your church has a Saturday evening or weekday worship service identical to Sunday morning worship. Some means of taking reservations is a key effectiveness element in the Consecration Sunday Stewardship Program.

- Some churches have rented a nearby facility such as a school gym or a civic center and scheduled a successful meal for 1,000 or more people after the third service.

- Other churches lack sufficient fellowship-hall space to seat everyone at the same time. However, if they are short only a few dozen seats, nearby Sunday school classrooms can sometimes handle the overflow. The Celebration Luncheon's only program element is the announcement of results by the Consecration Sunday chairperson. Thus youth, children, and a few adults can eat in classrooms.
- One church erected a tent on its grounds for a brunch following each of its four Sunday morning worship services.

Question: **How do we decide who to contact regarding Consecration Sunday attendance; in other words, how do we define "active" and "inactive"?**

Answer: "Inactive" means you have no record that this person worshipped in your congregation or made a "contribution of record" during the last year. Most churches prefer to get inactive people reconnected with church participation before they ask them for financial contributions. Otherwise, inactive people can say, "All they are concerned about is my money," a feeling you do not want to plant in their minds.

"Active" means you have a record of the person either attending at least once or financially contributing to your congregation at least once during the last twelve months. Yes, once a year for either behavior may seem to stretch the definition of "active." However, you do not want to send such people a signal of exclusion by not inviting them to an important church-family function. Use common sense. If contributing members live in Mexico City and your church is in New Jersey, send them all of the Consecration Sunday mailings, but do not ask someone to contact them for a Celebration Luncheon reservation the week prior to Consecration Sunday.

Question: **When do we build the proposed budget for next year?**

Answer: There is no proposed budget. You finalize next year's budget two weeks after Consecration Sunday as a result of the *fully completed* report sheet your financial secretary prepares. It includes four items: *(a)* the total of *Estimate of Giving Card* amounts, *(b)* the estimated loose offerings based on the last three year's average, *(c)* the total amount from people with consistent giving patterns during the last twelve months who were not present to complete an *Estimate of Giving Card*, and *(d)* all church income from non-donor sources such as interest, rentals, and fees.

There is no way that the total can be less than last year's operating budget, unless, of course, one or more large givers have moved away or are now deceased. Even then, new attendees and members who were not givers last year, along with the typical increases of an effectively executed *Consecration Sunday*, offset those losses.

Publishing a proposed budget prior to a stewardship campaign holds down the giving for several reasons. Instead of concentrating on the spiritual question "What percentage of your income is God calling you to give?" proposed budgets cause people to focus on the question "How much more does the church need this year than last year?"

Then, too, when you create and publish a proposed budget, you automatically set up a negative reaction. Few people in the church understand all of the line items. Everyone can look at the proposed budget and see two or three items about which he or she can say, "I don't know why we are spending money on that!" This creates an atmosphere of "How can we cut the budget?"—the opposite kind of atmosphere created by the spiritual question "What percentage of your income is God calling you to give?"

Additionally, a budget sets up in peoples' minds the feeling that you are asking them to give money to the church budget. Christian stewardship is not giving money to the budget; it is giving money to God. When we substitute the budget for God, we begin to destroy the biblical, spiritual teachings about generous Christian stewardship of all that God gives.

In large churches, of course, the committees can and must do some preliminary budget planning prior to Consecration Sunday. However, do not total the requests from various committees prior to Consecration Sunday. Wait until two weeks after completing the *Consecration Sunday Stewardship Program*.

Sunday, _____ (two weeks before Consecration Sunday): The Consecration Sunday team's Announcer #2 uses the "Grow One Step" in morning worship (available in the Download Library and shown on pages 90–91). Photocopy this as a two-sided sheet and fold one copy into each morning worship bulletin. (Or download those two pages from the Download Library and print them as a two-sided sheet.) Do *not* print your church's figures on the stair-step side of the sheet!

During oral explanation from the pulpit, Announcer #2 will ask worship attendees to write your congregation's figures in the blanks, so be sure the pew racks have plenty of pencils.

If your congregation regularly uses a projection screen during worship, you may want to download from the Download Library and use "Announcer #2: Optional PowerPoint Presentation," which contains numerous slides that match this oral announcement. If you use this optional PowerPoint presentation, do NOT print your congregation's figures on the stair step slide. However, DO replace each of the imaginary figures on each of the several slides that follow—using the statistics your financial secretary provides the previous week. If you wish to do so, you can personalize the presentation even more by adding a picture of your congregation to the lower-left corner of the slides and replacing the imaginary dates on the last two slides with the month and date of your congregation's Consecration Sunday and Celebration Luncheon.

The announcement unfolds as follows.

Announcer #2 begins with a brief personal witness, such as the following: "God has abundantly blessed my family, as I'm sure God has blessed your family, and we've always tried to be faithful stewards. So each year we ask ourselves, "How is God calling me to respond?"

For other personal witness ideas, see "Tips for Announcements, Teaching, and Sermons" on pages 65–72.

Whatever type of personal witness Announcer #2 makes, he or she must *not* stress the church's need for funds! He or she must *not* try to shame or guilt-trip people into generosity! Those approaches create negative results: anger and resentment toward the church and the announcer! The goals of this announcement are *(a)* to motivate each giver to grow spiritually by contributing a specific percentage of his or her income as a commitment to Jesus Christ, *(b)* to remind people that the Celebration Luncheon is not a potluck dinner, but a catered meal for which they make reservations, and *(c)* to invite everyone to complete a reservation card for the Celebration Luncheon.

"As we move toward Consecration Sunday two weeks from today, each of us will be thoughtfully considering our answer to the spiritual question, 'What percentage of my income is God calling me to give?' Please take the 'Grow One Step' sheet in your worship bulletin. Turn to the stair-step side of the sheet, and I'll give you some figures to write in the blanks. Starting at the lower left, write in this number: _____ [your church's financial secretary provided Announcer #2 these figures the previous week]. This means that _____ members of our church are not recorded as contributing to the financial support of the church's ministries during the last twelve months."

Announcer #2 moves up the stair-step chart, adding illustrations after each of the first three or four figures that he or she asks worship attendees to write on the stair steps. Examples: $5.00 to $9.99 equals a breakfast meal at McDonald's. $10.00 to $19.99 equals a movie ticket. $20.00 to $29.99 equals feeding a family of two or three at a fast-food restaurant. These illustrations powerfully demonstrate the value system people bring to their Christian stewardship. Do not continue the illustrations after the first three or four stair steps. They become less meaningful as you go up to larger dollar totals.

Announcer #2 then says, "Now, please turn over your sheet and look at the chart on the back. Let your eyes go down the left side of the scale until you come to your approximate salary level. Now move your eyes across to your weekly giving level to God's work through your congregation. Then move your eyes up to the top of the sheet to locate the percentage of your income that represents. During the next two weeks, I'm sure each of us will be pondering the question, 'What percentage of my income is God calling me to give?'" Announcer #2 continues by saying, "I'll now ask the ushers to come forward and distribute the *Consecration Sunday* reservation cards (sample shown on page 39). Our Celebration Luncheon is a catered meal, and we hope everyone will be there. As our musicians play some special music, I'll give you five minutes to complete your Reservation Card. Then the ushers will come back and pick up the cards. To be sure we leave no one out, we will make home visits to people from whom we do not receive a luncheon reservation card. So please help us by completing your card."

Announcer #2 pauses to give people time to fill out the cards.

Announcer #2 concludes with something like this: "In closing I would suggest that you consider doing the following: Turn the TV off, put the newspaper down, close your computer, pray, and ask God the question, 'What percentage of my income are you calling me to give to your work through this congregation?'" *Warning*: Do not place reservation cards in the worship bulletins or in the pew racks. Do not ask people to place them in the offering plates. All these methods sharply reduce the number of cards turned in, which sharply increases the number of personal contacts necessary during the week prior to Consecration Sunday.

Download from the Download Library the Reservation Card shown at the top of page 39. Personalize the dates to fit your church. Print on card stock.

Question: **Won't people feel uncomfortable with the "Grow One Step" sheet because it publicly labels their giving in comparison to other members?**

Answer: No church among the thousands that have used this procedure has reported such a response. Curiosity, interest, and

RESERVATION CARD

Consecration Sunday Reservation Card

I (we) will be present for morning worship and the Celebration Luncheon on Sunday, _____ (date).

____ Yes ____ No

The number of persons attending from my household will be _____.

Name _____

Telephone _____

---

personal reflection on the spiritual aspects of financial giving are the primary results of using the "Grow One Step" sheet in morning worship.

Question: We don't like side one [or side two] of the sheet. Why can't we just leave it out?

Answer: Both sides of the sheet are equally important. The two sides of the sheet appeal to the way two different types of people prefer to think about increasing their giving. Additionally, using both sides moves people from a "yes or no" decision to a "which of these two decisions do I prefer to make?"

Monday, _____ (two weeks before Consecration Sunday): Mail letter #2 (shown on page 41). Stick with the letter's basic outline. Change only the information needed to personalize it for your congregation. If possible, schedule this church leader dinner on the Sunday evening prior to Consecration Sunday. If that is not possible, schedule it no later than Monday evening.

Options: Some churches make this dinner complimentary and consider it one of the Consecration Sunday expenses. However, many churches ask each of the governing board members, committee chairpersons, ministry team chairpersons, church staff, and Consecration Sunday team members and the spouses of all these groups to pay for this dinner. The Consecration Sunday team makes this decision at its orientation session six weeks or more prior to Consecration Sunday.

Download Letter #2 from the Download Library and personalize the dates and church name. Print it on church stationery. *Note:* **Copyright permission is granted to use only in your congregation.** *Warning*: **Do not change words, add sentences, or delete sentences! Alterations risk damaging final results (significant increases in financial giving and the spiritual growth of donors).**

This letter may be sent as an email. However, if you choose to use email, please include a note in the subject line like, "Important email from your church: PLEASE open and read immediately."

Download the *Grow One Step* **meme from the Download Library and share it via your church's social media channels**

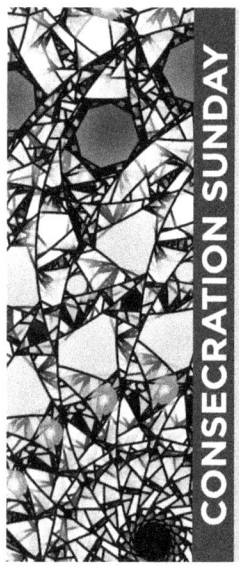

Question: **Couldn't we make this church leader dinner a potluck meal or ask a group in the church to prepare it?**

_____ [Dated Monday, two weeks before Consecration Sunday]

To: Church Governing Board Members, Committee/Ministry Chairpersons, Consecration Sunday Team Members, church staff, and the spouses of these groups. [List the names in a vertical column and on each letter place a red check mark by the name of the person to whom the letter is addressed.]

Ladies and Gentlemen:

I need your help in order to give our Consecration Sunday maximum spiritual impact among our congregation's members. We are not going to ask you to call in homes to obtain pledges from people, but your assistance in other ways is essential.

We are asking you to attend a dinner at ___ p.m., _____, [Sunday, or Monday of the week prior to Consecration Sunday], at _____ [a local restaurant—not at the church]. _____ [guest leader name] will bring a brief message regarding the spiritual-growth dimensions of stewardship in preparation for our Consecration Sunday.

Your attendance at this meal will strengthen the effectiveness of our stewardship emphasis and, thereby, our congregation's mission and ministry results for the coming year.

Sincerely,

Consecration Sunday Chairperson

Answer: Do not go that route. Scheduling this dinner at a local restaurant is the best approach. However, large congregations that regularly provide good food through a catering service or a kitchen staff can schedule this meal at the church if a restaurant setting seems unfeasible. Unlike the Celebration Luncheon on Consecration Sunday, asking the leaders to pay for their own meals does not damage the final financial results. However, this governing board dinner must not be a potluck or one that involves members in preparing the food.

Tuesday and Wednesday, _____ (two weeks before Consecration Sunday): The congregational governing board dinner telephone chairperson (someone who is pleasant and thorough in making all contacts) telephones all governing board members, church committee chairpersons, ministry team chairpersons, church staff, Consecration Sunday team members, and the spouses of all these groups, stressing the importance of their presence at the dinner for church leaders at _____ p.m., _____, _____ (day and date), at _____ (a local restaurant—not at the church), at which time _____ (name of your church's guest leader) will speak about the spiritual-growth dimensions of stewardship and the upcoming Consecration Sunday.

Friday, _____ (nine days before Consecration Sunday): Mail or email letter #3 (shown on page 44). Stick with the letter's basic content. Change only the information needed to personalize it for your congregation. *Change example*: A large church with multiple services may decide to modify the Celebration Luncheon procedure based on options suggested earlier in this timeline.

While mailed letters have often received the best results in the past, we are aware that email has become a way of life for nearly everyone. It is a fact that in the busy-ness of our present lifestyles, letters can unfortunately be laid aside and without some special reminder, emails may be placed on the back burner. If your church chooses to use an email approach due to the cost of mailed letters or lack of personnel to mail them, please include a note in the subject line like, "Important email from your church: PLEASE open and read immediately."

Download Letter #3 (shown on page 44) from the Download Library. Personalize the dates and church name. Print on church stationery. *Note*: **Copyright permission is granted to use only in your congregation.** *Warning*: **Do not change words, add sentences, or delete sentences! Alterations risk damaging final results (significant increases in financial giving and the spiritual growth of donors).**

Download the *Celebration Luncheon Reminder* **meme from the Download Library. Share it via your church's social media channels along with the following text: "Join us for worship and the Celebration Luncheon on Consecration Sunday, _____. [date]**

If you have not made a reservation, please contact _____[Consecration Sunday chairperson] to let us know you'll be there!"

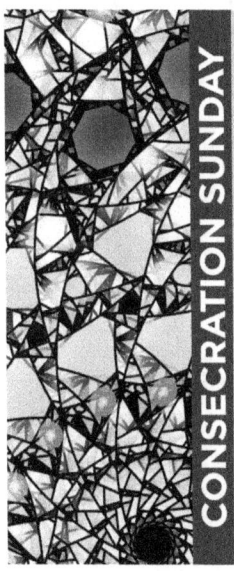

Detailed Road Map to *Consecration Sunday*

LETTER #3

_____ [Dated Friday, nine days before Consecration Sunday]

Dear Members and Friends of _____ Church:

You are by now surely aware that Sunday, _____, is Consecration Sunday for our congregation. We believe that you have sufficient concern for your spiritual growth and the mission and ministries of our congregation to attend the two special events of this day—Sunday morning worship and the Celebration Luncheon immediately following worship. This is a catered meal, so we need reservations for each person. If you have not finalized plans to attend these two events, please do so immediately.

Our goal is to have every member and regular worship attendee present. If you did not make a reservation during the last two weeks, please let us know that you will be present by calling or emailing the chairperson _____ [Consecration Sunday chairperson] at _____ [telephone number] or _____[email address]. The effectiveness of our church's mission and ministries next year depends on your initiative and dedication. Please make whatever sacrifices are necessary to be present on _____ [date].

Your servant in Christ,

Pastor

***Question:* Should we have sent Letter #3 a week sooner?**

Answer: No! We contact as many people as possible in worship and in person on two consecutive Sundays, not by letter, since more people respond affirmatively that way. This letter *(a)* is a safety net to make sure we do not leave someone out and *(b)* contains information to reduce the surprise factor among marginally active people we contact in personal ways during the five to three days prior to Consecration Sunday.

Sunday, _____ (one week before Consecration Sunday): The Consecration Sunday team's Announcer #3 makes a brief announcement in adult church school classes and morning worship regarding the importance of Consecration Sunday and the Celebration Luncheon on _____, _____ (day and date). Do not stress the church's need for funds! Do not try to shame or guilt-trip people into generosity! Those approaches create negative results: anger and resentment toward the church and the announcer! Stress each giver's need to grow spiritually by contributing a specific percentage of his or her income as a commitment to Jesus Christ. As part of the morning worship announcement, Announcer #3 includes a brief personal witness to his or her convictions regarding the value of financial stewardship. For ideas, see "Tips for Announcements, Teaching, and Sermons" (pages 65–72).

Remind worshippers that the Celebration Luncheon is not a potluck dinner but a catered meal for which they must make reservations. Repeat the Announcer #2 reservation card procedure from the previous Sunday, stressing the fact that if they filled out a card last Sunday, they should not fill out one today. Say the following: "I'll now ask the ushers to come forward and distribute the *Consecration Sunday* reservation cards. As our musicians play some special music, I'll give you five minutes to complete your card. If you already completed the reservation card last week, you may want to use this time for prayer and meditation on the question, 'What percentage of my income is God calling me to give?'"

"Shortly, the ushers will come back and pick up the cards. To make certain we leave out no one, we will make contact this week with people from whom we do not receive a luncheon reservation card. So please help us out by completing your card."

Warning: Do not place the cards in the worship bulletins. Do not place the cards in the pew racks. Do not ask people to place them in the offering plates. All these methods sharply reduce the number of cards turned in, which sharply increases the number of personal contacts necessary during the week prior to Consecration Sunday.

Sunday, _____ (one week before Consecration Sunday): The pastor preaches on the spiritual-growth value of Christian stewardship, emphasizing the tithe and percentage giving of income. Suggest the need to start somewhere, whether 5 percent or 6 percent or 7 percent—not as a legalistic rule, but as our response to God's love empowered by God's grace. See preaching resources listed on pages 70–72.

Sunday or Monday, _____, at _____ p.m. (two hours before the governing board dinner) held one week before Consecration Sunday: The guest leader meets at the church with the pastor, financial secretary, and Consecration Sunday team members. This checkup meeting finalizes plans for Consecration Sunday, especially to obtain luncheon reservations from those who have not yet made them. The guest leader also asks whether the financial secretary has calculated the last twelve months' giving patterns for each member, in readiness for quick tabulation of the *Estimate of Giving Cards* immediately following worship on Consecration Sunday—plus *(a)* the average total of loose offerings during the past three years and *(b)* the total church income from non-donor sources such as interest, rentals, and fees. In congregations that average fewer than 300 in morning worship, the financial secretary's failure to prepare these figures makes impossible the Consecration Sunday chairperson's announcement of the results at the end of the Celebration Luncheon.

Sunday or Monday, _____, at _____ p.m. (one week before Consecration Sunday): The guest leader speaks at a dinner for governing board members, committee chairpersons, ministry team chairpersons, church staff, Consecration Sunday team members, and the spouses of all these groups at a local restaurant. This speech *(a)* focuses on biblical and spiritual dimensions of financial stewardship, *(b)* emphasizes the tithe and percentage-giving of income, and *(c)* stresses the spiritual growth benefits of asking ourselves the question, "What percentage of my income is God calling me to give?" Humor, inspiration, and motivation are important elements in this speech.

After the speech, the guest leader asks the Consecration Sunday chairperson to distribute and read aloud a copy of the sheet printed on pages 48–49 titled "Instructions for Making Celebration Luncheon Reservation Contacts." (Change only those parts of the sheet that apply to local differences in the format, such as revisions of the Celebration Luncheon method in some large congregations.)

Download "Instructions for Making Celebration Luncheon Reservation Contacts" from the Download Library (shown on pages 48–49). Personalize the dates. Print on white or colored paper. *Note*: **Copyright permission is granted to use only in your congregation.** *Warning*: **Do not change words, add sentences, or delete sentences! Alterations risk damaging final results (significant increases in financial giving and the spiritual growth of donors).**

Assignments for Reservation Card Visits

The Consecration Sunday chairperson then makes assignments for Consecration Sunday reservation card visits. The goal is to contact all church members and regular worship attendees not present for morning worship the last two Sundays who therefore missed the opportunity to complete a reservation card. To accomplish these assignments in a small congregation, the pastor or Consecration Sunday chairperson calls out the names of the households "from which we do not yet have reservation

INSTRUCTIONS FOR MAKING CELEBRATION LUNCHEON RESERVATION CONTACTS

I. Our goal is to secure a promise from every church member and regular worship attendee to participate in Consecration Sunday by attending

   A. Morning worship on Consecration Sunday, _____ (date).
   B. The Celebration Luncheon immediately following worship that same day.

II. The visitor's goal is to get the member or worship attendee to attend. This does not include asking people for a financial commitment or being concerned about the amount they decide to give.

III. Accomplish your goal by the following steps:

   A. Each visitor makes a personal contact with every person on his or her list _____, _____, or _____ (the Monday, Tuesday, or Wednesday prior to Consecration Sunday). The visit informs people of the Consecration Sunday plan. People much more easily ignore, forget, or say no to a telephone contact. A home visit in which you ask them to attend always gets better results. Be certain to have lists made up for everyone with the addresses of all that you need to contact. Make a master list and be certain each visitor has a copy. Include on the list the email address for the chairperson.

   You may find it necessary to call or text those families that have not made reservations. A call or text message is better than no contact at all, but a home visit will get the best results.

   B. Emphasize the voluntary aspect of coming to the church for the morning worship and Celebration Luncheon on Sunday, _____ (date). Stress that their decision to financially support the congregation's mission and ministries is made in privacy as an act of worship.

   C. Stress that we want every member of the church to attend, even if they choose not to make a specific financial commitment.

   D. Use the reservation card to make their reservation for the Celebration Luncheon. Remember, people often resist the idea of making a reservation to go to church, so clarify that the reservation is for the luncheon.

IV. Telephone or email the Consecration Sunday chairperson and make a full report of your contact results by 7:00 p.m., _____, the Wednesday before Consecration Sunday (Thursday evening if the governing board, committee chairpersons, and Consecration Sunday team dinner is on Monday).

Assignments for Reservation Card Visits

The Consecration Sunday chairperson makes assignments for Consecration Sunday reservation card visits. The goal is to contact all church members and regular worship attendees not present for morning worship the last two Sundays who therefore missed the opportunity to complete a reservation card.

My name:_____

Names of members I will be visiting:

_____

_____

_____

_____

_____

_____

_____

_____

_____

_____

INSTRUCTIONS FOR MAKING CELEBRATION LUNCHEON RESERVATION CONTACTS

cards." Ask church leaders to raise their hands and volunteer to contact these people for the purpose of obtaining their reservations for the catered Celebration Luncheon on Consecration Sunday, _____ (date). The Consecration Sunday chairperson carefully records the names each church leader takes for contact.

In large congregations, accomplish these assignments by laying the reservation cards on a table at the front of the room, in alphabetical order. Ask the church leaders to come forward, one table at a time, and pick up the appropriate number of reservation cards. The chairperson records on a master sheet which cards they take.

Note: Invite staff members and spouses to this meal so that they can benefit from its educational and spiritual values, but do NOT ask them to make reservation contacts.

Monday, Tuesday, and Wednesday, _____, _____, and _____ (the week before Consecration Sunday): Governing board members, committee chairpersons, and Consecration Sunday team members make personal visits to obtain Celebration Luncheon reservations from people who have not yet made them. Brief, unannounced home visits cause far greater increases in the Consecration Sunday worship attendance—the primary goal of the contacts—than do telephone calls.

Thursday, _____ (before 7:00 p.m., the week before Consecration Sunday): All Celebration Luncheon reservations from personal contacts by governing board members, committee chairpersons, and Consecration Sunday team members are telephoned or emailed to the Consecration Sunday chairperson.

Thursday, _____ (after 7:00 p.m., the week before Consecration Sunday): The Consecration Sunday chairperson telephones all governing board members, committee chairpersons, and Consecration Sunday team members who have not called in the reservations they obtained and asks for their reports. If they have not finished their contacts, the chairperson asks that they complete them this evening and telephone him or her by 9:30 p.m.

Friday, _____ (the week before Consecration Sunday): The Consecration Sunday chairperson (and members of the Consecration Sunday team in large congregations) telephones for Celebration Luncheon reservations any members and regular worship attendees not contacted by the governing board members, committee chairpersons, and Consecration Sunday team members.

Sunday, _____ (Consecration Sunday): The guest leader preaches in morning worship and conducts a seven-minute commitment session at the close of the service. Through careful planning, control the length of the service to allow seven minutes for this closing commitment session. Do not plan to use a choral response of any kind at the end of the service. Craft the printed order of worship to conclude with "Commitment Time and Benediction, [name of guest leader]."

Completing the *Estimate of Giving Cards* has high spiritual meaning for people. After the service, ushers distribute the cards when the guest leader asks them to do so. The guest leader talks about the spiritual-growth significance of giving. Worshippers then complete the cards at their own pace. After finishing the cards, worshippers go forward informally, without being ushered or directed in any way, and place their cards on the Communion table or altar—providing that the church's architecture allows this. If the front of the church has steps that older people find hard to negotiate, at this point in the service, as the guest leader comes to begin discussing how to complete the card, an usher may place a small table on the floor level at the front of the sanctuary. This allows people of all ages to participate in this act of worship without climbing steps.

When the guest leader invites members and friends to fill out their *Estimate of Giving Card*, it is important to invite them to begin their new commitment period the week following Consecration

Sunday or as soon thereafter as possible. If people put off beginning their new commitment until January, a significant amount of the increase will be lost.

Question: Couldn't we just pass the offering plate and ask people to put their cards in them?

Answer: Going forward informally is an essential and important ingredient in the Consecration Sunday experience. Couples go forward together. Young families with children go forward together. What a marvelous teaching/learning experience this is for children! Often, worshippers are so spiritually moved that you see tears in some eyes as they leave the sanctuary on their way to the Celebration Luncheon.

Question: What about the worship visitors on Consecration Sunday who don't know what's going on?

Answer: They learn what is happening. The guest leader's explanation makes clear that this is a church family matter and they are not expected to fill out a card.

Question: May we photocopy (or reprint) the *Estimate of Giving Card* instead of buying them?

Answer: Permission is never granted to photocopy, change the wording of, or alter in any way the copyrighted *Estimate of Giving Card*. To do so is a violation of U.S. and international copyright law. Abingdon Press does not permit exceptions to this prohibition! No valid reasons exist for adding to or changing the card's wording. Positive experiences in thousands of congregations demonstrate that people have no difficulty understanding how to complete the *Estimate of Giving Card*.

Question: Why is the *Estimate of Giving Card* copyrighted?

Answer: Not for the purpose of selling cards, but to prevent well-meaning leaders of congregations from making changes that field-testing in thousands of congregations has found reduce the financial results of the program.

Question: **May we revise the wording on the *Estimate of Giving Card*?**

Answer: The urge to edit runs deep in church leaders, but when they succumb to the temptation to change the card, they often significantly reduce the financial results of the program. The sincere but misguided desire to improve the wording is a like a sincere, well-meaning, master carpenter who performs brain surgery. The carpenter may view the operation as a success, and the patient often dies.

Question: **May we print our church's name and address on the *Estimate of Giving Card*?**

Answer: Do NOT add to, subtract from, or make any changes whatever on this copyrighted *Estimate of Giving Card*. This change is as illegal a violation of copyright law as reprinting it without permission.

Question: **After the word "weekly" on the *Estimate of Giving Card*, may we add "monthly," "quarterly," and "yearly"?**

Answer: The card's line that says "per week" beside the dollar amount is NOT an accidental oversight. Experience indicates that if people prefer to state their giving intention on a monthly rather than on a weekly basis, they cross out "per week" and write "per month." If they prefer to write "per quarter," they do that.

But your guest leader and any other publicity should NOT tell them to do that. A "monthly" or "yearly" figure always looks larger to people than it actually is, especially to older people who began their giving patterns during pre-inflationary years. Yes, the word "weekly" requires people to think about this decision a bit more—but that is the point of an effective stewardship campaign!

Question: **May we print personalized donor information on the *Estimate of Giving Card*, such as a box for people to write in their Donor Number?**

Answer: Do NOT alter the *Estimate of Giving Card*. Do NOT put a box on the card for the donor households to write in their envelope numbers. This adds a complexity to the card that reduces the percentage of people who complete a card. Many of them mentally stumble, as they say to themselves, "I can't turn the card in today; I'll wait until I get home and find the envelope number; I'll turn it in later." *Result*: many of them never turn in the card.

Then, too, the envelope card number causes people to focus on the peripheral issue of "What is my envelope number?" instead of on the central question that makes Consecration Sunday get results, "What percentage of my income is God calling me to give?"

You are far wiser to invest more time in the tabulation process than to risk reducing the results toward which you strive in using Consecration Sunday, namely, *(a)* increased spiritual growth of your members and *(b)* increased financial support for your congregation's various ministries during the coming year.

Question: May we change the *Estimate of Giving Card* to allow a blank for designated gifts?

Answer: Permission is never granted to redesign the *Estimate of Giving Card* for multiple purposes, such as designated gifts or building-fund donations. You should do other kinds of campaigns separately, on a different date. If your church's long-term tradition *necessitates* a designation of money for two or more funds, the guest leader can mention this orally—at the time the ushers distribute the cards on Consecration Sunday morning—asking people to note on their cards a division of the total into those categories if they wish to do so. However, as soon as feasible, the stewardship committee or governing board should consider moving away from that practice—since it reduces the grand total that people give each year.

Question: May we redesign the *Estimate of Giving Card* to account for a congregation's tradition of using a two-pocket or a three-pocket method for designating annual giving to two or three different funds, such as "Operating," "Missions," and "Building"?

Answer: Churches usually began that tradition of what some call two-pocket or three-pocket pledging, hoping to increase total giving or to avoid the effort of multiple appeals. *However, there are more good reasons NOT to use that approach than to use it:* *(a)* Multiple-pocket cards, rather than increasing total financial giving, tend to hold down giving. *(b)* Multiple-pocket cards focus people on making a choice among funds rather than focus on the need of the giver to give for his or her own spiritual benefit. *(c)* Multiple-pocket cards focus people on dollar amounts rather than on the spiritual question, "What percentage of my income is God calling me to give?" *(d)* Multiple-pocket cards encourage people to make choices based on information they do NOT possess. The congregation's governing board has a much greater ability to see the most appropriate way to disburse funds—in light of overall congregational goals and needs. *(e)* Multiple-pocket cards encourage that short list of people—when they get irritated with a pastor or something that happens in the church—to exercise their anger in inappropriate ways, such as designating their total annual giving to mortgage reduction and giving nothing to the operating fund. Congregations should avoid any system that makes possible unhealthy types of decisions.

Question: **May we redesign the *Estimate of Giving Card* to make more prominent the blank where people write in the dollar amount?**

Answer: The design of the *Estimate of Giving Card* causes people to focus on the spiritual question, "What percentage of my income is God calling me to give?" instead of on the accounting question of a dollar amount. People who engage themselves in this card's process have no difficulty in finding the blank to write in the amount. And their response to that spiritual question, "What percentage of my income is God calling me to give?" produces far larger dollar amounts for the church's ministries!

Question: **May we redesign the *Estimate of Giving Card* so that it focuses more on the total amount of money we need for our proposed annual budget?**

Answer: Fear of not focusing on the budget is usually an anxiety that stems from changing to "unfamiliar methods" instead of "familiar methods that we used last year." This natural reaction is far more emotion-based than rationally based. You can overcome this anxiety by saying, "Let's try this new approach and see how it works." After church leaders use this program and the *Estimate of Giving Card* once, they become fearful of returning to the old approach that did not work as well!

Question: **May we redesign the *Estimate of Giving Card* so it doesn't emphasize the word *tithe* so much?**

Answer: Permission is never granted to alter the *Estimate of Giving Card* in that manner. People know that *tithe* is a biblical word and they are not offended by it, even though they have never practiced it, or prefer not to practice it. The word may seem negative to some leaders; it is not negative in the minds of church members.

Sunday, _____ (Consecration Sunday): Immediately after worship the financial secretary and an assistant go to the church office. They use the previously prepared computations of the past twelve months' giving patterns for each household, the *Estimate of Giving Card* that people turned in during worship, and a calculator or spreadsheet to fill in the blanks of the "Statistical Report on Consecration Sunday Results" (available in the Download Library, shown on page 58).

The objective is to hand this report sheet—with every blank filled in—to the Consecration Sunday chairperson so that he or she can read the results to the Celebration Luncheon attendees by the end of the meal.

After the Consecration Sunday chairperson reads the report, the Celebration Luncheon attendees sing the "Doxology" to conclude the celebration.

Question: **How can we accurately compare the giving from last year with the anticipated giving for next year if we had gigantic designated gifts last year or lost some big givers?**

Answer: Meticulously complete all the blanks in the "Statistical Report on Consecration Sunday Results" (available in the Download Library, shown on page 58). Do not include designated gifts in the three totals, since they are not the objective of the Consecration Sunday program. However, if your church traditionally uses two-envelope or three-envelope commitment cards, you should include the total giving pattern, not just the operational section of your two- or three-envelope system.

If one or more large givers from last year are no longer present in the church, you may want to identify that fact as a footnote in your report by saying something like this: "We have achieved these results despite the fact that several major donors from last year have moved away or are now deceased." This puts the results into a rational perspective.

Download from the Download Library the "Statistical Report on Consecration Sunday Results" (shown on page 58). Print on plain paper for completion by the financial secretary. *Warning*: Unless every blank is filled in, this report is not a valid picture! Read this in its entirety as an oral announcement at the Celebration Luncheon and/or read this from the pulpit the following week and/or print it in the church newsletter one week later.

Monday, _____ (the day after Consecration Sunday): Mail letter #4 (shown on page 59) to households that did not attend the Consecration Sunday worship service. Include a stamped, self-addressed, return envelope and an *Estimate of Giving Card*. Type or write on each card the name and address of the person(s) receiving the letter. Personalizing the card in this way greatly increases the number of cards returned. Avoid sending this letter to people who attended on Consecration Sunday but did not complete an *Estimate of Giving Card*.

Download Letter #4 (shown on page 59) from the Download Library. Personalize the dates and church name. Print on church stationery. *Note*: Copyright permission is granted to use only in your congregation. *Warning*: Do not change words, add sentences, or delete sentences!

STATISTICAL REPORT ON CONSECRATION SUNDAY RESULTS

A total of _____ giving units (husbands and wives or single persons) completed *Estimate of Giving Cards* this year.

A total of _____ of these giving units increased their financial commitment above their last year's amount.

A total of _____ giving units present to fill out *Estimate of Giving Cards* today committed a total of $_____.

Based on last year's giving records, we can expect to receive $_____ during the coming year from people who have consistent giving patterns during the past twelve months but are not present today.

Based on the average total of loose offerings during the past three years, we can expect to receive $_____ during the coming year from that source.

Church income from non-donor sources such as interest, rentals, and fees is expected to be $_____.

This gives us a grand total of $_____ anticipated income for the next twelve months.

The total income for our general operating budget during the last twelve months was $_____.

Next year, we can expect our operating budget income to increase by $_____.

This is a _____ percent increase in total giving above last year.

LETTER #4

_____ (Dated the Monday after Consecration Sunday)

Dear Christian Friends:

We had a great crowd and excellent response during our Consecration Sunday yesterday. We regret that you could not be with us, but we know you will want to participate in the financial support of your church during the coming year.

We have therefore enclosed your *Estimate of Giving Card*. Could you help us to complete the campaign by returning it this week?

Thanks for your help in bringing this fine spiritual experience to a good conclusion.

Sincerely,

Consecration Sunday Chairperson

Monday, _____ (one week after Consecration Sunday): Mail (do not email) a personalized letter of thanks to each household that completed an *Estimate of Giving Card*. In this thank-you letter, state the exact dollar amount of the household's weekly or monthly commitment. Include in the letter one to three examples of ministries that their gift makes possible and an example of lives that this generosity will change for God and good.

Due to perceived confidentiality issues in some congregations, this letter should come from the financial secretary. It is widely known in congregations that the financial secretary has access to all giving records and records the giving from week to week.

Download the *Thank You* meme from the Download Library. Share it via your church's social media channels, along with the following text: "Thank you to the members of _____ [church name] for making a commitment on Consecration Sunday! Your generous support of God's work in our congregation will change lives and our community in extraordinary ways."

Question: **Isn't this thank-you letter unnecessary?**

Answer: The thank-you letter serves four important purposes. They are: *(a)* a personal word of thanks is always appreciated; *(b)* the thank-you letter reinforces donors' decisions to increase their giving; *(c)* the thank-you letter reminds donors that their giving makes a difference; and *(d)* the thank-you letter contains the amount that they wrote on the *Estimate of Giving Card*—which they will not otherwise have—and a written reminder that the approximately 30 percent of donors who are forgetful and detail-challenged sorely need.

Question: **Shouldn't we do more follow-up to get cards from people who usually give but did not turn in a card?**

Answer: Absolutely not! You said in the publicity that you would not do this. If you do any more follow-up, people will not believe what you tell them next year. Experience indicates that such contacts (instead of or in addition to the recommended letter on Monday following Consecration Sunday) do not increase the actual amount of dollars that year by more than 1 percent. You are much better off, long term, when you help people to develop the habit of bringing their contribution commitments to God's house instead of chasing them down. Asking them to voluntarily make spiritual commitments as an act of worship also helps to explain why in the average stewardship program across the United States, congregations collect 93 percent of the pledges, whereas congregations that use Consecration Sunday collect 98 percent to 102 percent of the amount people write on their cards. Finally, the financial secretary has already counted them at last year's giving level. The only amount you would be missing is the increase they might have given.

> **The Bottom Line:** If you followed the instructions in this chapter to the letter, everyone wins. The congregation wins! You win! God wins! Congratulations!

Additional Questions Unrelated to the Timeline

The following questions are frequently asked by leaders of congregations that are considering or have recently conducted Consecration Sunday.

Question: **Can we do Consecration Sunday and then at another point in the year do a capital-funds campaign for facilities construction or improvement?**

Answer: Yes, but separate them by about four months.

Question: **Our church's centennial (or some other special Sunday) is coming up at about the same time we usually do our annual stewardship campaign. Can we combine that with Consecration Sunday?**

Answer: Don't do it! You reduce the effectiveness of both.

Question: **Can we use Consecration Sunday for other purposes, such as a debt-retirement campaign, or a building campaign, or to make up a budget shortfall this year resulting from an inadequate operating fund campaign last year?**

Answer: Don't do it! Each of those needs requires a completely different approach. Do not use Consecration Sunday for any purpose other than your annual operating campaign. It works extremely well for that purpose but for that purpose only.

Question: **What if one or two of our laypersons feel quite negative about the Consecration Sunday Stewardship Program?**

Answer: Such a reaction is not unusual. Typically, this is caused by *(a)* poor personal stewardship habits, *(b)* fear that the program will succeed and prove his or her negative predictions wrong, *(c)* fear of personal loss of control when the church has sufficient resources, or *(d)* fear of change. This sometimes happens with one or two individuals the first year the congregation uses Consecration Sunday. It seldom happens during the second or subsequent years. In all likelihood, those same individuals may well object to any stewardship program you elect to use.

Research Fact: Approximately 5 percent of members in every congregation are prone to unhappiness regarding virtually ANY change a church makes in any aspect of its mission and ministry methods. When that happens, smile and nod, and do what you feel God is calling you to do.

Question: **How should a large congregation prepare its budget?**

Answer: In large congregations, building next year's budget usually involves several months of effort. Leaders should base budgets on vision and goals. The committees must begin to decide what they think God is calling them to do in their particular section of church life by dreaming, visioning, and thinking. After that they should ask, "What does it cost to do what needs to be done?"

Ordinarily, a good procedure in large churches is to have the committees work out their budget needs and turn them in to the finance committee—which totals up all the budget requests from the various committees. Sometimes the budget committee must go back to one or more of the committees and ask them to rethink some of their requests in light of the overall goals of the church and the total available resources. Sometimes this requires consultation with individual committee chairpersons. But if your stewardship levels are increasing in the way they can increase when you use *Consecration Sunday* for several consecutive years, such rethinking is more the exception than the rule.

Whatever system you elect to use for budget preparation in a large church, involve a large number of leaders in the process over a period of two or three months. When more people own the budget at early stages, fewer people object to it later.

Question: **Should the pastor have access to giving records?**

Answer: Most congregations have formal or informal rules and traditions that govern who can know the amount people give. Many churches permit three people to know. One is the financial secretary. Another is the governing board chairperson or finance chairperson. The third is the pastor, since a person's financial giving is as much a spiritual matter as is his or her worship attendance. Use whatever rules your congregation or denomination has established in this matter. Some congregational leaders are fearful that if the pastor knows everyone's giving, he or she will tend to favor those who give the most in pastoral services. Such a situation is rare. In this writer's experience, the opposite is true. If a poor giver is hospitalized or has a special need, they are more likely to get attention from the pastor in accordance with those needs.

Tips for Announcements, Teaching, and Sermons

Your personal theological and giving convictions, expressed through the unique gift of your personality, are more powerful than any canned appeal. However, as you develop what you say, the following tips keep you focused on what best motivates the thinking, feelings, and spiritual convictions of most church members.

Talk about financial stewardship from perspectives that motivate people to give generously, not from perspectives that motivate people to give selfishly. The five primary motivators of people in high per capita giving congregations are as follows:

1. They feel gratitude to God.
2. They see giving as part of their spiritual relationship with God.
3. They feel privileged to serve.
4. They feel that God asks for an appropriate percentage of their income.
5. They like to help other people.

Other motivators are influential causes of financial giving among a few church members, but not many. Low per capita giving churches base their financial appeals on these seven:

1. They want to help their church.
2. They see giving as a duty.
3. They feel that giving adds meaning to life.
4. They give out of habit.
5. They feel guilty if they do not give.
6. They feel or fear God's judgment if they do not give.
7. They give because of social/peer pressure.

Most motivational experts teach that leaders do not actually motivate anyone from the outside. Rather, leaders create a set of circumstances that cause people to behave in ways that match the motivations already present in their minds and hearts. On which motivator list—the top five or the bottom seven—have your congregation's operating-budget efforts focused during the last few years?

Talk about the need of givers to give for their spiritual benefit, not about the need of the church to receive so it can pay its bills. The first appeal concentrates on the five strongest motivators. The second appeal focuses on the seven weakest motivators.

Instead of asking, "What does our church need to balance its budget?" ask, "What percentage of your income is God calling you to give?" Contrary to popular opinion, young-adult givers respond even better than older-generation givers to this spiritually focused approach to stewardship.

Assume that people can enjoy rather than feel negative about the annual stewardship program. That is always true with a properly executed Consecration Sunday Stewardship Program since its principles and procedures connect with their personal motivations for giving.

Talk about financial stewardship from a biblical perspective, not from a budget-balancing perspective. The Bible teaches that people who take seriously the stewardship of all that God gives them have these characteristics: They give through the church (Malachi 3:10), liberally (Luke 6:38), sacrificially (2 Corinthians 8:1-4), cheerfully (2 Corinthians 9:7), and regularly (1 Corinthians 16:2). We find nowhere in the biblical record instruction for giving to the church budget. We find abundant texts that urge people to give to God.

Instead of talking about tithing and percentage giving in legalistic or judgmental ways, talk about these behaviors as a personal faith commitment for which God's grace empowers us.

Regardless of what annual stewardship program their churches choose, effective pastors and lay leaders teach and preach financial giving in ways that are biblical and spiritual without being legalistic or judgmental.

Examples of a layperson's announcement/personal witness:

1. "It would be hard for me to say that this church needs my money. I'm only one of a large number of members. The budget is sizable. The church will not go under without my money. But the central issue of financial stewardship is not the church needing my money. Giving brings me a sense of meaning, joy, and spiritual growth in my relationship with God that nothing else does. The central issue of financial stewardship is my need to give. Remembering that reminds me what our annual stewardship program is all about: focusing on what I think God is calling me to give, not on what the church needs to receive."

2. "Why do I believe in financial stewardship? My biblical and theological beliefs are foundational to my convictions about Christian giving. Three of these theological convictions are especially important. First, I believe in Jesus Christ, and I believe that Christ has the greatest potential to change the lives of people of anything they can take hold of. Second, I believe in the church. I believe the church is the body of Christ and has tremendous potential for changing and improving and enriching people's lives. Third, I believe in stewardship. Financial giving enables a church to do what God calls it to do to help people and to serve Christ, and financial stewardship helps individual Christians to grow spiritually. So as we travel through the weeks leading up to our Consecration Sunday, let's not lose sight of why we are doing this. In so many ways, it is a marvelous opportunity for each of us to grow spiritually and by so doing help to grow God's ministries in our congregation and community."

3. "Without voting to do so or realizing it, over the past several decades the leaders in many churches have

substituted secular fund-raising methods for Christian stewardship procedures. Fund-raising for nonprofit organizations in the community is as different from Christian stewardship as a bicycle is from an eighteen-wheeler. Both are valid forms of transportation, but they are not interchangeable. They accomplish two different goals.

"The goal of secular fund-raising is to raise dollars for a worthy cause. The goal of Christian stewardship is the faithful management of all that God gives, so that God can use our gifts to transform us spiritually and to reach out to others with Christ's transforming love. The apostle Paul spells out those two goals in the lengthy definition of stewardship in his letter to the Corinthians (2 Corinthians 9:11-14 ESV).

"You will be enriched in every way to be generous in every way, which through us will produce thanksgiving to God. For the ministry of this service is not only supplying the needs of the saints but is also overflowing in many thanksgivings to God. By their approval of this service, they will glorify God because of your submission that comes from your confession of the gospel of Christ, and the generosity of your contribution for them and for all others, while they long for you and pray for you, because of the surpassing grace of God upon you.

"Jesus summed up the spiritual connection between money and God this way: 'Where your treasure is, there your heart will be also' (Luke 12:34). Financial stewardship is treasure management that helps us to escape the trap of selfishness by keeping ourselves spiritually focused on God. We frequently hear the question asked in this text, 'Where does your treasure lie?' It's not a bad question, but a more spiritually focused question would be, 'Where do I want my heart to be?' If we put our treasure there, our heart will follow."

"That is what John Wesley meant when he said that if people were more alive to God, they would be more generous. Each of us makes one of two choices in life. We either become emotionally attached to our money, or we become emotionally attached to the God who gives us our money. Although we often hope to do both, in our heart we know that cannot happen. Financial stewardship helps us to overcome the temptation to break the first commandment and put the false idol of money first, ahead of the God who revealed his love for us through Jesus Christ."

"Our annual stewardship campaign is much more than fund-raising. It also helps each of us to grow spiritually in our relationship with God through the faithful management of all that God gives us."

Example of a pastor's sermon segment one week before Consecration Sunday: This approach avoids the danger of talking about giving in a judgmental or legalistic way, while stimulating people to think of financial stewardship in spiritual rather than merely monetary terms.

> "Our annual stewardship Sunday is coming next week. As we prepare for that important spiritual decision, each of us will be reflecting on the question, 'What is God calling me to give as a percentage of my income?' That is a personal, spiritual question, and three kinds of people answer it in three different ways."

> "Some people answer it by saying, 'I feel God is calling me to give 10 percent of my income to the Lord's work. I have been thinking about tithing for several years, and I want to begin that spiritual journey this year.'"

> "Another kind of person responds to the question like this: 'Eventually, I want to begin tithing, but I am not ready to do that this year. I feel God is calling me to start somewhere—to drive my tent pegs in the ground at 5 percent or 6 percent or 4 percent—knowing that God will bless that decision by helping me to increase my giving in coming years.'"

> "A third kind of person has been tithing for many years. For example, one couple said years ago when they were just getting started, 'We'll tithe now; later we'll do more.' The years rolled by and now they say, 'Wow! Do we ever have more! So much more that we cannot fathom how we arrived at such a high annual income that 10 percent does not even come close to a sacrifice for us. We feel God is calling us to give 15 percent or 20 percent of our income to the Lord's work.'"

> "*Forbes* magazine once told about Hugh and Nancy McFarland, Jr., who had been giving away 70 percent of their income for eighteen years, since Hugh was thirty-nine (*Forbes*, December 15, 1997). Should the McFarland's pastor have limited stewardship teaching to a 10 percent concept? Probably not!"
>
> "As we prepare for our annual stewardship Sunday, I know each of us will be praying for God's guidance as we prepare to answer the spiritual question, 'What percentage of my income is God calling me to give?'"

This kind of preaching and teaching, reinforced by effective stewardship methods, leads congregations beyond legalism, beyond judgmental statements, and beyond secular fund-raising tactics. This approach produces positive responses and high levels of per-member financial giving by making the giving of money a spiritual issue that fits different household income levels.

The following resources may be helpful as you prepare to give a personal witness or preach on stewardship: *One-Minute Stewardship*, by Charles Cloughen, Jr. (Church Publishing, 2018) contains short reflections that can be included in weekly emails, bulletins, and newsletters, or read during worship. *Just in Time! Stewardship Services*, by David Mosser (Abingdon, 2007) contains material for twenty-four worship services including suggested liturgies, prayers, Scripture passages, and sermon helps to aid preaching, teaching, or brief announcements.

Sermon preparation and teaching resources: The Bible is the best resource. Dipping into it for sermon material helps pastors get over their natural reluctance to urge members to become good stewards. Someone noted that the word *believe* appears in the Bible 273 times, *pray* appears 371 times, and *love* appears 714 times. *Give* appears 2,172 times. In fact, Jesus talked about money more than any other subject except the kingdom of God itself. Finding a good sermon text is not a big challenge.

The word *steward* is derived from the Anglo-Saxon word *sty-warden* and from the Greek word for the manager of a household—*oikonomos*. The Bible contains twenty-six direct references to "steward" and "stewardship."

In the Hebrew Scriptures, *Asur-beth* means servant, a supervisor or foreman who must make decisions, give orders, and take charge. Stewards are usually accountable to a royal personage, such as a king or ruler. In the Bible's first use of the term (Genesis 43 and 44), *steward* appears in the story about Joseph, a Hebrew prisoner promoted by Pharaoh to high rank in Egypt.

The New Testament Greek word *oikonomia* is translated "stewardship." This is a combination of two words: *Oikos*, meaning "house," and *nemo*, meaning "to divide, distribute, or apportion." *Oikonomia* has various meanings in classical Greek, but its most direct reference is to the administration or management of a household. *Oikonomos*, which is translated "steward," often referred to a slave who was given responsibility over money, property, goods, or other slaves. *Oikonomos* (steward) appears twenty times in the New Testament. *Epitropos*, a word referring to a trustee, appears three times. *Oikonomia* (stewardship) appears seven times. However, many teachings regarding stewardship occur in both the Old and New Testaments apart from the actual usage of stewardship words.

This picture of a servant-manager of something or someone not belonging to him- or herself is the most obvious meaning of the New Testament passages Matthew 20:8; Luke 8:3; and John 2:8. But the idea also begins to take on theological and metaphorical meanings. In Luke 12:42-48 (ESV), "steward" or "manager" and "servant" are used interchangeably. Stewardship and watchfulness are characteristic marks of Christ's true followers. The Pauline and other epistles, written later in the first century, shift to an almost doctrinal use of the Gospels' parabolic treatment of stewardship. In 1 Corinthians 4:1-2 (ESV), Paul applies the concept of "steward" explicitly to himself as an apostle and implicitly to the church at large.

Travelogue of Stewardship Preaching and Teaching Scripture:

Exodus 25:2—Giving with willing heart

Exodus 36:2-7—Giving to the Lord in overabundance

1 Chronicles 29:3-4—Personal treasures given to temple

1 Chronicles 29:14—Giving back to God what God has given to us

Psalm 37:21, 26—Giving generously

Psalm 50:23—Value of sacrifice and offering

Psalm 54:6-7—Giving out of gratitude for deliverance

Psalm 112:5—Blessings on generous people

Proverbs 3:9-10—Honor the Lord with one's wealth

Proverbs 22:9—Blessing for the generous

Malachi 3:8-10—Stealing from God

Matthew 5:23-24—Giving with clean heart

Matthew 6:2-4—Private stewardship

Matthew 6:19-21—Treasures on earth and treasures in heaven

Matthew 23:23—Fullest measure of giving

Mark 4:24-25—Those given much and those given little

Mark 12:13-17—Paying taxes to government

Mark 12:41-44; Luke 21:1-4—Widow's small offering

Luke 3:11—Sharing with others

Luke 6:38—Abundance repays those who give

Luke 12:33-34—Selling one's possessions for the poor

Acts 10:2—Devout centurion

1 Corinthians 4:2—Need to prove faithful

1 Corinthians 16:2—Giving on first day of week

2 Corinthians 8:1-5—Persecution brings overflowing joy and generosity

2 Corinthians 9:6-7—Sowing and reaping

2 Corinthians 9:10—God rewards givers

Galatians 6:6—Student sharing with teacher

Hebrews 13:16—Share with others

1 Peter 4:10—Using one's gifts for the good of others

Beyond Second-Year Use of *Consecration Sunday*

Unlike most other annual stewardship campaigns, many congregations across the United States have reported using *Consecration Sunday* for seven or more consecutive years with significant increases in total congregational contributions each year. However, boredom is the root of much evil in church life. Beyond the second year, leaders face three major dangers.

1. As with most other kinds of church programs, leaders who become familiar with how to execute *Consecration Sunday* are tempted to eliminate some of the parts. Often the part they chop out is a key element in producing its effectiveness. Thinking they are trimming toenails, they remove the heart and lungs.
2. Leaders are tempted to discard *Consecration Sunday* because "we have done that and need to do something else," not realizing that it continues to produce large increases in total church giving each year.
3. Leaders are tempted to skip doing any kind of annual stewardship campaign, hoping to coast on *Consecration Sunday's* momentum or assuming that no further increases can occur for several years.

Those fatal misjudgments can be overcome in these ways: *(a)* retain determination to use the principles of *Consecration Sunday* and *(b)* use slight variations after the first two years that help parishioners feel they are doing something different. The following are examples of cosmetic variations.

Morning Worship Lay Witnessing: During the four weeks prior to Consecration Sunday, ask four laypersons to give a three-minute witness to their faith during morning worship. Ask them to speak out of their personal experiences and convictions regarding the reasons for and benefits of growing spiritually through financial stewardship. Do *not* try to shame or guilt-trip people into generosity! Those approaches create negative results: anger and resentment toward the church and the speaker! Do not say "We need to balance the church budget." or "The church needs the money." Rather, talk about the spiritual benefits of giving.

Stewardship Study/Discussion Procedure for Adult Classes and Small Groups: During the weeks prior to Consecration Sunday, engage adult classes in a study of stewardship.

Example of a one-session adult class study: Print the following Scriptures on a single sheet of paper and distribute to class members or to all adult classes meeting together in a joint session. Ask people to count off by numbers, using a number that, when divided by four, includes everyone in the room. (This ensures that spouses and close friends seated together end up in different groups.) Ask people to find their group (#3s are in one group of four; #4s are another group of four, and so on).

1. "No one can be loyal to two masters. He is bound to hate one and love the other, or support one and despise the other. You cannot serve God and the power of money at the same time" (Matthew 6:24 JBP).
2. "If anyone wishes to be a follower of mine, he must leave self behind; he must take up his cross and come with me. Whoever cares for his own safety is lost, but if a man will let himself be lost for my sake, he will find his true self. What will a man gain by winning the whole world, at the cost of his true self? Or what can he give that will buy that self back?" (Matthew 16:24-26 NEB).
3. "I tell you this," [Jesus] said: "this widow has given more than any of the others; for those others who have given had more than enough, but she, with less than enough, has given all that she had to live on" (Mark 12:43-44 NEB).
4. "Don't let the world around you squeeze you into its own mold, but let God re-mold your minds from within, so

that you may prove in practice that the plan of God for you is good, meets all his demands and moves toward the goal of true maturity" (Romans 12:2 JBP).

5. "This is how one should regard us, as servants of Christ and stewards of the mysteries of God. Moreover it is required of stewards that they be found trustworthy" (1 Corinthians 4:1-2 RSV).

6. "Remember: sparse sowing, sparse reaping; sow bountifully, and you will reap bountifully" (2 Corinthians 9:6 NEB).

7. "For it is the nations of the world that strive after all these things, and your Father knows that you need them. Instead, strive for his kingdom, and these things will be given to you as well" (Luke 12:30-31).

8. "On the first day of every week, each of you is to put something aside and store it up, as he may prosper, so that there will be no collecting when I come" (1 Corinthians 16:2 ESV).

9. "Give, and it will be given to you; good measure, pressed down, shaken together, running over, will be put into your lap. For the measure you give will be the measure you get back" (Luke 6:38 RSV).

10. "Each one must do as he has made up his mind, not reluctantly or under compulsion, for God loves a cheerful giver. And God is able to provide you with every blessing in abundance, so that you may always have enough of everything and may provide in abundance for every good work" (2 Corinthians 9:7-8 RSV).

Ask each group of four people to select a recorder. The overall session leader asks each group to work with only one of the Scriptures. Each group interacts with its assigned Scripture in the following ways:

1. Spend five to ten minutes discussing what this Scripture means for Christians today.

2. Next, give all four individuals in each group a slip of paper. Ask them to write in their own words, without discussing it with others, the answer to this question: "If you had to express the meaning of this Scripture in your own words, how would you say it?"
3. After five minutes each group recorder collects the slips of paper. The session leader asks the recorders to report to the entire class how their group interpreted its assigned text and to read the slips of paper aloud. The session leader then closes by saying, "We now have a room full of experts on the meaning of Christian stewardship."

Ten-Year ABCs for Stewardship and Finance Committees

Churches that use the following principles for three to ten years continue to see significant annual increases in their total offerings.

A. High per capita giving congregations move beyond the illusion that Christians automatically commit themselves to generous financial stewardship. Many pastors graduate from seminary with the conviction that they will preach the gospel with such compelling power that people will respond enthusiastically, the money will come in, and church finances will take care of themselves. Strong stewardship levels, like every other aspect of Christian discipleship, require education, repeated decisions, and continued personal growth. Annual and year-round stewardship education helps to accomplish that goal.

B. High per capita giving congregations move beyond the illusion that high worship attendance equals strong financial stewardship. "If we get the people there, the money will come," leaders often quip. "If the people are in church and the crowds are good, the money will take care of itself." Anyone who has served as church financial secretary knows the inaccuracy of that old cliché. If you get the people there and they are five-dollars-a-week people, or if they are still giving at a 2007 level of income, the money does not come. Growth in stewardship does not automatically result from increased worship attendance. In fact, the opposite is true. Large congregations often have lower per capita giving than smaller ones.

C. High per capita giving churches delete from their conversations the myth that "our people are giving all they can." Research indicates that at most, 26 percent of churchgoers consistently give 10 percent of their incomes to God's work through their congregation ("USA Snapshots," *USA Today*, February 23, 2000). Few if any congregation's members are at the red line—in danger of giving too much.

D. High per capita giving congregations understand that people give to causes such as United Way for a different reason than they give to their congregations. United Way is an excellent organization with high motives. But United Way focuses on fund-raising. By necessity it puts a budget together that meets the annual needs of supported organizations. However, that procedure does not achieve maximum contributions from church members. "How much money does the church need?" is a natural question, but it is basically a bill-paying, fund-raising question. Better questions: "How much money does God call me to give? What percentage of my income does God ask me to contribute?" Paul tells the Corinthian Christians to give as they have prospered. As God has blessed us, we are to give. Those ideas more closely match the motivations behind why church members give.

E. High per capita giving congregations understand the morale-building value of strong financial stewardship. A small congregation wanted a full-time pastor, but could not afford one. The church had never had a stewardship campaign. At first they resisted, but they eventually relented and scheduled one, driven by their dream of a full-time pastor. The first year they used *Consecration Sunday*, their contributions increased 36 percent. They achieved their dream of a full-time pastor.

Can you imagine the difference in atmosphere in that congregation? The same change happens in congregations where meetings are no longer dominated by questions such as, "Can we really afford to do that?" or "How are we going to pay the bills?" What a different feeling when people are asking, "How will we use this money God is giving us?" A better financial picture puts a happy face on congregations. It makes the family much more fun to live with.

F. High per capita giving churches recognize that few people increase their giving unless the church asks them to consider an increase annually. Most stewardship increases come from the "stimulus-response" principle. If churches do not change the stimulus, they keep getting the same response.

Seldom is someone who is driving down the street toward the grocery store overcome by the spiritual conviction, "I need to increase my giving to the church." Thus, most people tend to remain at the same giving level, even when their incomes increase.

As well as damaging them spiritually, that behavior damages their church financially. As inflation increases church expenses, especially at the point of skyrocketing health insurance for pastors and energy costs for heating and cooling the building, small congregations can no longer afford a full-time pastor. Midsize and larger churches find their ministries strangled due to lack of financing.

G. High per capita giving congregations conduct a stewardship campaign of some kind every year. What makes the greatest difference in personal stewardship levels in congregations? Not the median income of the county; some churches in the top ten per capita income counties in the United States have the lowest per capita contribution level in their denominations. Not the median income of the church members; people with high incomes do not necessarily contribute generously. Not regular church attendance; people can attend worship every week and give at incredibly low levels. One thing, and one thing only, causes high per capita giving: The presence of an effective annual stewardship program.

Churches with poor or nonexistent annual stewardship programs inevitably fall into a lower giving pattern because they use a dues-paying mentality or a bill-paying mentality instead of a stewardship mentality. The leaders in a small-town congregation expressed their pride in not having stewardship campaigns of any kind like this: "When we need the money, people always come through." These leaders should have been embarrassed instead of proud. Their Mayday method (S.O.S.—the ship is sinking) is not Christian stewardship; it is a bill-paying, dues-paying, fund-raising mentality that blocked members from a significant spiritual growth experience and kept the congregation's mission and ministry in poverty.

Ironically, by insisting that they do not want to talk about money in the church, that church's leaders guaranteed that money would be the topic of conversation at every board and committee meeting. In discussing every new idea, the question, "Can we really afford to do that?" replaced the question, "What is God calling us to do?"

A few people who are old enough to remember the abuses of pledges in the desperate days of the Great Depression of the 1930s contribute mightily but refuse to put their intentions on paper. However, 95 percent of people who say, "I'll give, but I won't pledge" are really saying, "I'll give, but I won't give much."

"What time of year should the annual stewardship campaign happen?" a pastor asked. When it happens is not as important as what happens; quality is more important than time of year. However, due to the natural pattern of seasons and budgeting processes, 69 percent of churches conduct their stewardship campaigns during September, October, or November; 26 percent conduct their campaigns in December, January, or February; 3 percent choose March, April, or May; and only 2 percent conduct them in June, July, or August (Ben Gill, *The Joy of Giving: The Nature of Spiritual Giving* [Dallas: Myriad Communications, Inc., 1994], p. 5).

H. High per capita giving churches concentrate on the need of the giver to give rather than on the need of the church to receive. The first is a stewardship procedure; the second is a dues-paying or bill-paying approach that tends to hold giving down rather than lift it up.

I. High per capita giving churches avoid focusing their stewardship appeals only on that section of the membership that gave little or nothing during the past few years. Most congregations are far below the potential giving level of their most capable households. The following statistics approximate the giving patterns in most churches.

- Five percent of the contributors give 25 percent of the church budget.

- Ten percent of the contributors give 25 percent of the church budget.
- Twenty percent of the contributors give 25 percent of the church budget.
- Sixty-five percent of the contributors give 25 percent of the church budget.

Since those figures also approximate the distribution of wealth in the United States, most of the people in the 5 percent group are as capable of increasing their giving as the people in the 65 percent group.

Among Americans who regularly attend worship, around 35 percent do not give a regular amount, 20 percent give round dollar amounts ($10, $20, and so on), 6 percent give a certain percentage of income but not 10 percent, and 26 percent of worshippers give 10 percent of their income ("Churchgoers Pass the Plate," *USA Today*, August 28, 2000). Effective annual stewardship campaigns change those percentages.

J. High per capita giving churches base their stewardship appeals on a biblical foundation rather than on an institutional or budget-building foundation. People do not give to church budgets for the same reasons that they give to United Way. A biblical, spiritual, and theological foundation is essential for high stewardship levels in local churches.

Rick Warren, pastor of the fastest-growing Baptist congregation in history, puts it this way: "We easily miss the spiritual-growth significance of giving money. We need to give the first part of our day in meditation to God. We need to give the first part of our week in worship of God. We need to give the first part of our income to God. We need to give the first part of our social life to fellowship with other Christians. Each of these four kinds of giving keeps our mental compass focused in God's direction. Remove any one of them and spiritual growth slows" (Rick Warren, *Discovering Spiritual Maturity* audiotapes, C.L.A.S.S. 201, Saddleback Valley Community Church, Orange County, California).

K. High per capita giving churches encourage their pastors to provide theological and methodological leadership for the annual stewardship campaign. On commercial airliners many crew members play important roles. The pilot, however, plays a particular role without which all other roles would become irrelevant. He or she must know how to find the destination airport and safely deliver the passengers to it. Likewise, the pastor's leadership in stewardship is a key aspect of his or her pastoral role, and no one else can play it. When a pastor says, "Money is not my thing," that is like saying, "Preaching, or prayer, or worship, is not my thing." One of the pastor's major roles is to build mature disciples. Stewardship is a fundamental part of our spiritual relationship with Christ. Authentic discipleship does not exist without it.

Pastors cannot wait until people grow spiritually so they will give generously. Some people cannot grow spiritually until they decide to give generously. Jesus said, "Where your treasure is, there your heart will be also" (Luke 12:34). Some people cannot get their hearts in the right place until they make a decision to put their money in the right place. Many people report making a decision during their congregation's annual stewardship program that took down a spiritual-growth roadblock they had not known was there.

Yet many pastors are uneasy talking about tithing and percentage giving for several reasons: *(1)* fear that people will be irritated; *(2)* fear of appearing to interpret Scripture in a legalistic way; *(3)* fear of coming across as judgmental instead of as pastoral and caring; *(4)* fear that people might think they are talking about money as a way of promoting an increase in their own salary; and *(5)* fear that they will have to examine their own personal giving pattern.

Pastors overcome these anxieties when they believe Ashley Hale's assertion that "The giver is the principal beneficiary of the gift," a slightly revised version of Jesus's suggestion that it is more blessed to give than to receive. Pastors also understand that tithing and percentage giving help people to grow spiritually and have experience with annual stewardship programs that treat financial giving as a spiritual rather than as a fund-raising matter.

L. High per capita giving churches encourage their pastors to teach and preach the biblical teachings of percentage giving of income and tithing. Many pastors who give effective stewardship leadership preach financial stewardship sermons twice a year. They are careful to avoid preaching on money only when the church is in a financial crunch and at the time of the annual stewardship campaign. Pastors who fall into that pattern warp financial giving into a crisis response or a bill-paying matter instead of a spiritual issue.

Preach stewardship sermons without warning (do not give advance publicity in the newsletter), but at appropriate times of the year. Try to avoid what a pastor in Arkansas did. He announced that he would preach on stewardship the following Sunday. The church was comfortably filled—meaning that each worshipper had room to lie down in the pew and take a nap. The preacher announced that he had changed his mind about the text of the sermon and preached on the prodigal son and the good Samaritan. Six months later, on Easter Sunday, the sanctuary was filled to capacity. He rose to speak and said, "Brothers and sisters, I have changed my mind with regard to the sermon topic." He then delivered a strong sermon on tithing. After the service, concerned elders called a meeting. They felt he had taken undue advantage of the unsuspecting crowd.

Most laypersons know that giving is part of the biblical message. St. Francis of Assisi is attributed with saying, "Preach the gospel at all times. If necessary, use words." You can also use dollars, and laypeople know that they are serving God with their financial giving as much as if they were preaching sermons from behind a pulpit.

Everywhere in Scripture we hear the warning: Money has power. Wealth is addictive. Be careful. Stay on your guard. It can replace God as your god. Someone who counted Scripture verses claims that Jesus talked about the use of money more than he talked about sin or love or prayer. If Jesus talked about the spiritual significance of money, why should his present-day apostles not talk about it?

People who put their financial commitment on paper give, on average, twice as much as people who do not. But people who make commitments based on a percentage of their income give three times as much as those who base their decisions on a dollar amount. Giving is a learned behavior. People tend to give or not give according to what their congregations and denominations ask them to give. Thus, 73 percent of Assemblies of God members tithe (give 10 percent of their income to God's work through their church); 44 percent of Southern Baptists tithe; 9 percent of Lutherans tithe; 7 percent of Presbyterians tithe; and 4 percent of Catholics tithe ("A Crisis in Giving," *Dallas Morning News*, January 13, 1996). Congregations that use dues-paying and bill-paying methods get what they ask for (dollars). Congregations that teach Christian stewardship get what they ask for (a percentage of members' incomes). Asking for a percentage of income produces three times as many dollars as asking for dollars.

M. High per capita giving congregations have pastors who witness to their personal beliefs and practices about financial giving. Among all denominations, 63 percent of pastors give at least 10 percent of their before taxes income to God's work. Yet one out of three pastors do not tell their congregation, thereby missing a great influence opportunity (Leith Anderson, *Leadership That Works* [Minneapolis: Bethany House Publishers, 1999], p. 131).

N. High per capita giving churches involve numerous laypersons in executing the annual stewardship program. The more people the church involves in doing something on a personal basis, the greater will be its increase in giving. However, in effective annual stewardship campaigns, that personal involvement does not consist of asking laypeople to make home visits to ask people to sign a pledge card.

O. High per capita giving churches recognize that laypersons do not like to visit other laypersons and ask them directly for money. People in small churches and small towns have special anxieties at this point. Their fear of asking often increases beyond the bearable because they are asking friends and relatives about personal financial issues. This is one of the reasons why many smaller congregations and churches in small towns disdain every kind of stewardship program. Because they have never heard of any kind of stewardship campaign other than visiting people to ask for pledge cards, they refuse to run the risk of damaging important personal relationships.

But this anxiety is present to some degree in churches and communities of every size. Thus, congregations need an effective annual method that asks people to revisit their financial stewardship decisions but does not require them to verbally confront one another concerning those decisions. (Capital campaigns for refurbishing or constructing facilities are an exception to this rule. In those endeavors, people expect and benefit from one-on-one visits that give them opportunity to ask questions and to learn about the project.)

P. High per capita giving churches rely on proven step-by-step, how-to-do-it programs rather than asking a committee to design the annual stewardship program. Stewardship is one of those disciplines in which, if people are left to their own devices, they always choose what seems to them like the easiest way (and therefore the least effective way) to do the annual stewardship campaign. Stifle the temptation to invent your own stewardship campaign. Find a published program that has proven itself in other churches. Do it by the book, no shortcuts.

Invent-it-yourself models are used by church leaders who (*1*) get bored with one of the models that works and/or (*2*) prefer to believe that financial stewardship programs do not work and/or (*3*) are too lazy to use annual stewardship programs and/or (*4*) do not believe that stewardship is part of personal spiritual growth and/or (*5*) think themselves intellectually or theologically superior to people who develop and field-test the programs that work. Invent-it-yourself models hold financial giving at minimum levels and foster the development of spiritually immature Christians.

Q. High per capita giving congregations complete the annual stewardship campaign before they complete and present the church budget. Contrary to the conviction of many individuals and finance committees regarding stewardship, a well-constructed budget gives people no good reasons for generous giving and countless excuses for not giving. Distribute a proposed budget in a roomful of church board members and you create a roomful of experts on how to trim the budget. Someone says, "Why are we spending money on this?" Someone else says, "We could save some money by dropping that. It probably doesn't do much good."

Publicizing the budget first puts a lid on total giving for another reason: Many members, automatically remembering the "fair share" motto of many secular organizations, make minor increases in their giving when they see that the new budget is only 3 percent or 5 percent higher than last year's.

Building the budget *after* the campaign takes the lid off potential increases (*1*) by eliminating the "my fair share" syndrome, (*2*) by eliminating the inevitable negative reaction everyone has to one or two items in the printed budget proposal, and (*3*) by building a biblical foundation on which high-percentage increases appear each year instead of building a ceiling above which giving will not rise.

R. High per capita giving congregations understand that four weeks is the maximum length for an effective annual stewardship program. In the old days of the 1960s and 1970s, people tolerated some of the twelve-week programs devised by their denomination's national stewardship departments. Now, sustaining attention for that period of time is an impossible dream. When the annual campaign goes beyond four weeks, minds wander. People become bored. Some learn from this long program that "All we ever do is talk about money." Be bright, be brief, and be done works best with this generation of hyper-busy adults.

S. High per capita giving congregations make changes in their annual stewardship campaign every three years. Same old, same old sends the mind to the sandman. Thus, congregations that use most of the commercially published programs must change to a different one after two years. While research proves that the Consecration Sunday Stewardship Program is an exception to this rule, slight variations in its execution after the first two years help to maintain its effectiveness. Changes get attention and facilitate better decision-making—thereby stronger spiritual growth. With your minor changes, however, avoid abandoning the proven principles in these stewardship ABCs.

T. High per capita giving congregations discuss time/talent stewardship during a different month than they schedule the annual financial campaign. Talking about money and time/talent at the same time causes some people to treat them like a multiple-choice question. "I'll give time instead of money" is an inappropriate spiritual decision. Congregations should never create the impression that they are offering that kind of choice.

U. High per capita giving congregations use different methods for their annual operating budget campaign than for capital improvement campaigns. People give to operating budgets from a pocket marked "current income." A great many capital-campaign gifts, especially the largest ones, come from a second pocket labeled "accumulated resources."

The leaders of high per capita giving churches use three different methods in asking people to reach into their second pockets to fund the following three kinds of capital improvements. *(1)* To accomplish a small missions or capital improvement project, members often respond to a general appeal letter. *(2)* Larger capital improvement projects usually require a highly organized, internally led "Miracle Sunday" type of campaign, which has raised amounts between one-third and three times the size of the church's annual operating budget in countless congregations across the United States.

V. High per capita giving congregations provide year-round stewardship education opportunities. Occasional three-minute personal witness by different laypersons during the worship services strengthens giving habits.

Just in Time! Stewardship Services by David Mosser (Abingdon, 2007) contains liturgies, prayers, suggested Scriptures, and sermon helps to plan worship focused on stewardship.

Many churches report benefiting from special four- to eight-week courses using study resources, such as material developed by Crown Ministries (www.crown.org) or the books and studies found at Horizons Stewardship (horizons.net/resources).

W. High per capita giving congregations use print witnessing to remind people of the spiritual value of giving. They frequently print church newsletter articles and provide other materials that stress percentage-of-income giving and tithing, rather than appealing to "the need for generous giving to help our church balance its budget." *One-Minute Stewardship* by Charles Clougher, Jr. (Church Publishing, 2018) contains short reflections that can be read in worship or included in weekly newsletters, emails, or bulletins. Additional inexpensive educational/motivational booklets are available from the stewardship departments of most denominations.

A pastor in Pennsylvania reported printing this phrase in all worship bulletins and newsletters: "Join the tithing fellowship." That spot commercial influenced stewardship thinking and behavior patterns even though nothing else was said about it.

X. High per capita giving congregations have stewardship and finance committees that provide year-round educational and motivational leadership. A book that stewardship committees can read and discuss, one chapter at a time, during their monthly meetings throughout the year is *Generous People: How to Encourage Vital Stewardship* by Eugene Grimm (Nashville:

Abingdon, 1992) often available through Amazon. Others include *The Generosity Challenge* by Scott McKenzie and Kristine Miller (Abingdon, 2019) and *God vs. Money* by J. Clif Christopher (Abingdon, 2018).

Y. High per capita giving congregations do not let one or two influential laypersons that resist annual stewardship campaigns amputate their church's health and effectiveness. Some resisters had a bad experience in past years with a poorly led or poorly structured stewardship program. Other resisters base their negative convictions on a bad experience in which laypersons were asked to visit the homes of other laypeople and ask for pledges. Often, however, people who most strongly resist scheduling an annual stewardship campaign are embarrassed about their own giving level. They do not want to participate in a program that causes them to rethink their own commitment.

Z. High per capita giving congregations understand that an annual stewardship campaign never fails. People do not stop being Christians between one year and the next year. One of the most dependable mental reflexes in church life is "Put me down for the same amount as last year." Even in the most poorly designed and miserably executed stewardship campaigns, a few households will increase their giving. The others will continue to give what they did the previous year. Thus, no kind of campaign totally fails. Unless several major givers die or move out of town, the congregation always has more income than it had prior to the campaign.

GROW ONE STEP CHART — BREAKDOWN

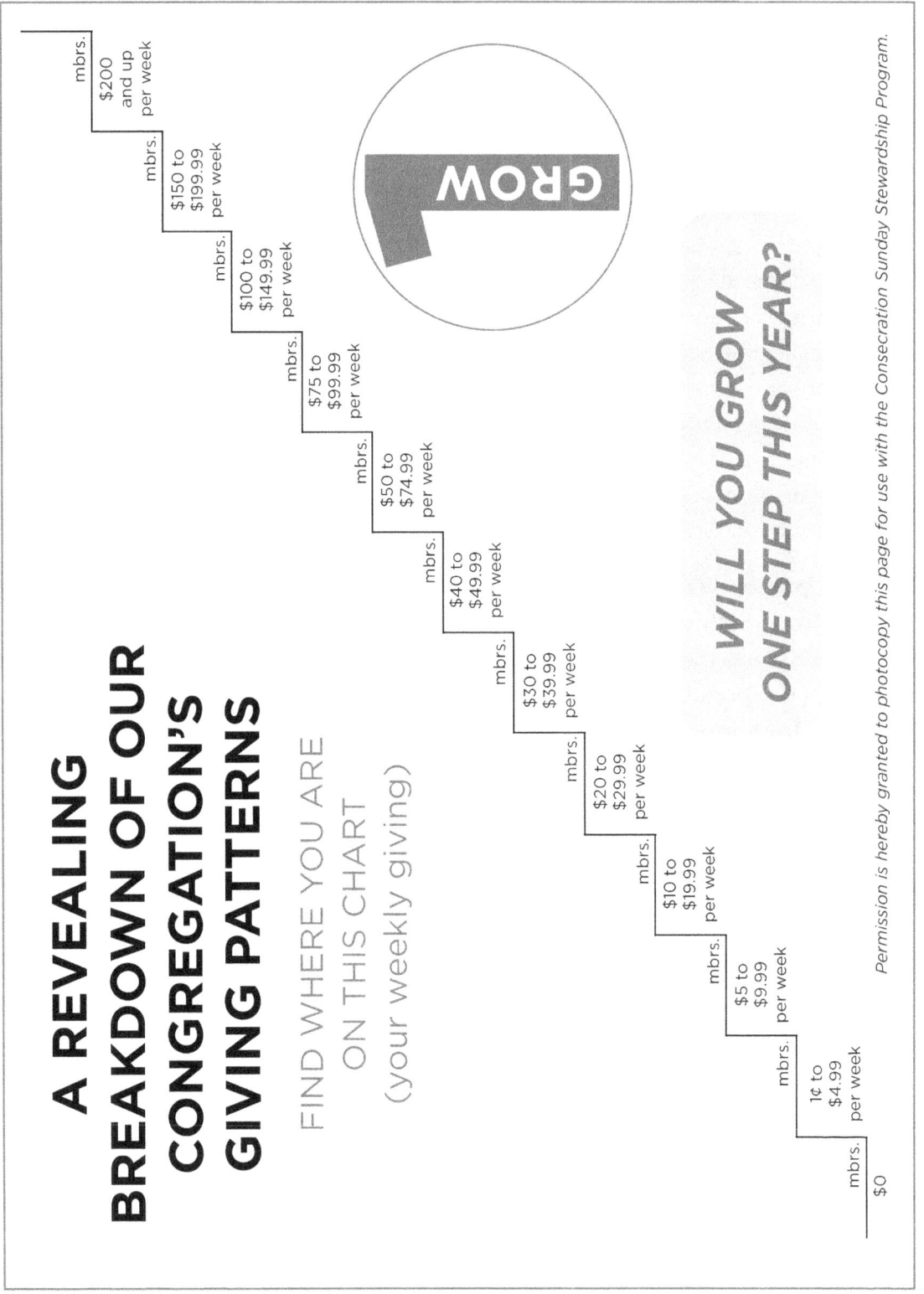

A REVEALING BREAKDOWN OF OUR CONGREGATION'S GIVING PATTERNS

FIND WHERE YOU ARE ON THIS CHART
(your weekly giving)

- ___ mbrs. $200 and up per week
- ___ mbrs. $150 to $199.99 per week
- ___ mbrs. $100 to $149.99 per week
- ___ mbrs. $75 to $99.99 per week
- ___ mbrs. $50 to $74.99 per week
- ___ mbrs. $40 to $49.99 per week
- ___ mbrs. $30 to $39.99 per week
- ___ mbrs. $20 to $29.99 per week
- ___ mbrs. $10 to $19.99 per week
- ___ mbrs. $5 to $9.99 per week
- ___ mbrs. 1¢ to $4.99 per week
- ___ mbrs. $0

WILL YOU GROW ONE STEP THIS YEAR?

Permission is hereby granted to photocopy this page for use with the Consecration Sunday Stewardship Program.

GROW ONE STEP CHART — WEEKLY INCOME/GIVING %

WEEKLY INCOME	BEYOND A TITHE		TITHE	UPPER RANGE GIVING				MIDDLE RANGE GIVING				LOWER RANGE GIVING		
	15%	12%	10%	9%	8%	7%	6%	5%	4%	3%	2%	1%		
$200	30.00	24.00	20.00	18.00	16.00	14.00	12.00	10.00	8.00	6.00	4.00	2.00		
$300	45.00	36.00	30.00	27.00	24.00	21.00	18.00	15.00	12.00	9.00	6.00	3.00		
$400	60.00	48.00	40.00	36.00	32.00	28.00	24.00	20.00	16.00	12.00	8.00	4.00		
$500	75.00	60.00	50.00	45.00	40.00	35.00	30.00	25.00	20.00	15.00	10.00	5.00		
$600	90.00	72.00	60.00	54.00	48.00	42.00	36.00	30.00	24.00	18.00	12.00	6.00		
$700	105.00	84.00	70.00	63.00	56.00	49.00	42.00	35.00	28.00	21.00	14.00	7.00		
$800	120.00	96.00	80.00	72.00	64.00	56.00	48.00	40.00	32.00	24.00	16.00	8.00		
$900	135.00	108.00	90.00	81.00	72.00	63.00	54.00	45.00	36.00	27.00	18.00	9.00		
$1000	150.00	120.00	100.00	90.00	80.00	70.00	60.00	50.00	40.00	30.00	20.00	10.00		
$1100	165.00	132.00	110.00	99.00	88.00	77.00	66.00	55.00	44.00	33.00	22.00	11.00		
$2000	300.00	240.00	200.00	180.00	160.00	140.00	120.00	100.00	80.00	60.00	40.00	20.00		
$3000	450.00	360.00	300.00	270.00	240.00	210.00	180.00	150.00	120.00	90.00	60.00	30.00		

1. Find where YOU are on the chart (your weekly income/giving).
2. Move one block to the left to determine what GROW ONE % would be for you.

Permission is hereby granted to photocopy this page for use with the Consecration Sunday Stewardship Program.

Ten-Year ABCs for Stewardship and Finance Committees

NOTES

NOTES

NOTES

NOTES

NOTES

Guest Leader Guide

Guest Leader Guide

A congregation has selected you as its guest leader for *Consecration Sunday*. Even if you have never handled this role before, your results will be as great the first time you lead it as the tenth time—providing you carefully study and meticulously follow the instructions.

Ten Steps to Guest Leader Effectiveness

If you have led (*a*) other types of stewardship programs or (*b*) an earlier version of Consecration Sunday, delete those methods from your mindset. *Consecration Sunday* uses very different principles and methods than other stewardship programs. This edition of *Consecration Sunday* improves on earlier editions of *Consecration Sunday* by using the feedback from thousands of congregations and hundreds of conversations with guest leaders.

Step #1: Obtain your own copy of this book, the *Consecration Sunday Stewardship Program Guide with Download Library* (the "Guest Leader Guide" is included). In most cases, the congregation where you are to serve as guest leader provides you with a copy. If not, get it by calling 800-672-1789, by visiting Cokesbury.com, or by requesting from the congregation where you are to serve as guest leader. Also, check to be sure the church you are assisting has followed the instructions for securing the other materials listed on page 14.

First, read pages 5–91 of this book. Then, read this "Guest Leader Guide" section of the book. Reading these materials will prepare you to begin the journey toward an effective Consecration Sunday experience that (*a*) helps attendees grow spiritually and (*b*) adequately finances their congregation's mission and ministries.

Step #2: Obtain—or ask the congregation in which you serve as guest leader to obtain—an appropriate number of *Estimate of Giving Cards*

from 800-672-1789 or by visiting Cokesbury.com. Under no circumstances should you permit the congregation you lead to mail or distribute the cards in advance of Consecration Sunday or prior to the end of the worship service that day.

Experience indicates that the wisest procedure is for the congregation to order the cards, have them shipped to the guest leader, and ask him or her to bring the cards on Consecration Sunday. This protects the congregation and the guest leader from the ever-present danger of Murphy's Law spoiling the results.

Step #3: Before you make the first visit to conduct the Consecration Sunday team orientation session six weeks or more prior to Consecration Sunday, make sure the church's governing board has voted to do *Consecration Sunday*. This protects you from arriving to meet with the team and learning that you are expected to "sell" the board or the finance committee on the program the same night you are trying to explain how to use it.

If you learn that the church has not yet voted to use *Consecration Sunday*, ask the leaders to read pages 5–8 of this book and/or to suggest that you—or someone from a congregation that has used the program—come and speak with the appropriate decision-making group. Explain that after they make their decision you will be ready to come for an orientation session with the Consecration Sunday team that the governing board or finance committee has appointed.

Step #4. During the orientation session—on the first of the three visits you will make to serve as guest leader—a major part of your role is to help the Consecration Sunday team select the appropriate options for their size congregation. *Consecration Sunday* works in churches of every size, denomination, and theological persuasion. Churches that have never conducted any type of stewardship campaign, churches that have had bad experiences with procedures in which people visit each other's homes and ask for pledges, megachurches, microchurches, and midsize churches have reported excellent results.

The congregation's size and number of worship services determine a few elements of how its leaders apply *Consecration Sunday* principles, such as reservations for the Celebration Luncheon. Each of these options is listed in the program explanation pages of this book. Common sense and conversations during the guest leader's orientation session easily arrive at the appropriate selection of options.

Step #5: Six weeks or more prior to Consecration Sunday, schedule a one-hour orientation session with the Consecration Sunday team appointed by the congregation's governing board or finance committee. Unless the congregation has already purchased and had shipped to you sufficient copies of the *Consecration Sunday Stewardship Program Guide* (the older versions of this program are outdated), order the books (bill them to the church) and take them with you to the orientation meeting. Effectively accomplishing the orientation session is impossible unless each of the team members and the pastor is holding a copy of the book in his or her hand. In addition to the copy you need as guest leader, the church needs two copies of the *Consecration Sunday Stewardship Program Guide* (one copy for the pastor and one copy for the Consecration Sunday chairperson) and seven copies of the *Consecration Sunday Stewardship Team Member Manual* (one for each of the other seven members of the Consecration Sunday team).

Do not send the books in advance of the meeting! Do not fill in the timeline dates on each book. However, *do* fill in the timeline dates on your personal copy. (In a telephone conversation with the pastor prior to the orientation meeting, agree on the appropriate Consecration Sunday date.)

After handing each team member a book, read through appropriate sections aloud—word-for-word—asking them to write in the blanks the dates that you give them. Read the letters as you come to them on the timeline, as these provide an effective, brief overview of the program. Do *not* read the *Question and Answer* sections, unless a team member or the pastor brings up a concern in that section of the timeline.

On the timeline pages (pages 19–20) that lists the persons on the Consecration Sunday team, stop and ask who will fill each of those roles. Fill in the blanks with the names. Resist the idea of having any one person take more than one of the roles. If you do not have eight people present in the room, urge the group to recruit other people to fill the remaining roles during the next few days.

When you come to the "Statistical Report on Consecration Sunday Results" (*to be completed by the financial secretary*), **stress to the team and the financial secretary the absolute necessity of carefully preparing in advance the figures for several of these blanks.**

Prepare an excel spreadsheet with the following columns. It will make the final tally both accurate and easy. The financial secretary fills in the first three columns. When tallying the results first fill in column four. Then for those not attending, fill in column five if, and only if, there is no number in column four.

Names (last name first)	Giving Last 12 Months	Giving per Week Last 12 Months	New Estimate of Giving	Expected Giving if No Estimate Provided	Running Total

- The blank that shows giving for the last twelve months means exactly that. Rather than taking an income report from the previous budget year, total the giving from the last twelve months—starting with last month's treasurer's report.
- The financial secretary also must bring to Consecration Sunday a list of the total dollars given by each giving

unit for the most recent twelve months. This allows for a quick check-off of giving units present and speedy tabulation of totals for giving units not present on Consecration Sunday.
- The financial secretary also must bring to Consecration Sunday:
  (a) the average total of loose offerings during the past three years, and
  (b) the total church income from non-donor sources, such as interest, rental, and fees.

Make these statements *in the presence of the entire team*, not just to the financial secretary in private. Otherwise, the occasional passive-aggressive financial secretary who prefers that his or her church not do this type of stewardship program may scuttle the process by not showing up with the figures necessary to give a full and accurate report at the Celebration Luncheon on Consecration Sunday.

Instruct the financial secretary in the presence of the entire Consecration Sunday team to be ready to start computations in the church office at the close of morning worship on Consecration Sunday. A computer or calculator and at least one helper make possible timely completion of the tabulation. In small and mid-size churches (up to 300 average worship attendees), a well-prepared and well-organized financial secretary can hand the report to the Consecration Sunday chairperson to read at the end of the Celebration Luncheon. In larger churches, the financial secretary must complete the report later, for announcement the following Sunday morning and in the church newsletter.

Emphasize to the financial secretary, in the team's presence, the necessity of completing every blank on the form. Otherwise, the Consecration Sunday chairperson cannot read any of the report because partially reading it distorts the results and creates inaccurate impressions in parishioners' minds.

Suggest that the Consecration Sunday team not schedule a program at the Celebration Luncheon, unless it is very brief—such as not more than one or two specials by a youth choir. The day's program was morning worship, the commitment session, and reading the results report by the Consecration Sunday chairperson. The Celebration Luncheon is the climax of the day, not the prelude to another program. Remind the team that their church will probably use *Consecration Sunday* again in future years. Keep people in the building for a long luncheon program, and you risk reducing attendance on similar Sundays in years to come.

Step #6: Meet with the Consecration Sunday team two hours prior to the governing board dinner on Sunday or Monday evening before Consecration Sunday. This meeting accomplishes several critical functions:

- If the reservation cards for giving units that have not yet made Celebration Luncheon reservations (which the Consecration Sunday chairperson will distribute at the dinner two hours from now) are not prepared, sufficient time remains to accomplish that.
- If the financial secretary does not have the advance financial data prepared for the giving units in order to quickly complete the tabulation on Consecration Sunday, publicly reviewing that necessity usually motivates him or her to take action. This reminder, stated in the entire team's presence, protects the team from embarrassing consequences when the Consecration Sunday chairperson is ready to read the report at the end of the Celebration Luncheon one week from now.
- If any other confusion or unexpected problems have arisen, the guest leader has time to help smooth them out.

Step #7: Speak at the dinner for governing board members, committee chairpersons, ministry team chairpersons, church staff, and the Consecration Sunday team and the spouses of all these groups on Sunday or Monday evening one week prior to Consecration Sunday.

This speech (*a*) focuses on biblical and spiritual dimensions of financial stewardship, (*b*) emphasizes the tithe and percentage giving of income, and (*c*) stresses the spiritual growth benefits of asking ourselves the question, "What percentage of my income is God calling me to give?" Humor, inspiration, and motivation are important elements in this speech.

Step #8: Serve as guest preacher in the morning worship service(s) on Consecration Sunday. Talk about the biblical and spiritual dimensions of financial stewardship, emphasizing the tithe and percentage giving of income. Stay relaxed, remembering that meticulously doing the details of *Consecration Sunday* cause the results, not the content of your sermon. By Sunday morning, most members have already decided what they intend to write on the *Estimate of Giving Cards*—before they arrive at worship.

Resist pressure to send the *Estimate of Giving Cards* to the church in advance. Say that everyone needs to be present to fill out the cards on Sunday. Anyone who cannot attend that day will get the opportunity to do so the following week. Letting people fill out cards in advance reduces the attendance at and the climactic nature of Consecration Sunday.

The best system, as noted in Step #2, is for the guest leader to bring the cards with him or her on Sunday. This prevents tragic accidents, such as arriving at the church to discover that someone placed the cards in the pew racks or the worship bulletins or mailed them with letter #3 last Friday.

When you arrive at the church on Sunday, talk to the Consecration Sunday chairperson and/or the head usher about the necessity of not handing out the cards until you call for them at the end of the service.

Step #9: For the seven-minute time of commitment at the end of morning worship on Consecration Sunday, go down to the sanctuary's floor level. Say something like the following:

- "If you are a visitor here today, don't be uncomfortable. This commitment service is something our

- congregation does once a year. If you are a visitor, we invite you to stay for the meal. We have arranged extra plates for visitors."
- "If you are a member and do not wish to complete an *Estimate of Giving Card*, we do not want you to feel pressured to do so. We do hope you will consider this, but it is a totally voluntary process."
- "I will now ask the ushers to distribute an *Estimate of Giving Card* to each household giving unit while I make a few comments about the commitment process in which we are engaged."
- "When we leave the sanctuary, we will go directly to the fellowship hall" (or to whatever meal site the church uses; a few large churches find it necessary to serve the meal at a nearby school, armory, or other location). "The food is being prepared for us right now. There will be no delay in serving. Please begin eating as soon as you sit down. I will say a blessing with my prayer before you bring your cards forward.
- "Each time we celebrate the Lord's Supper—Holy Communion—we take in our hands a small piece of bread made without yeast and a small cup with wine or grape juice. During those moments, these common elements symbolize the deepest meanings of our faith. During the next few minutes when we take an ordinary pencil and a small card, these symbolize the high and holy commitment we make in response to the love God has given each of us." [Leaders in various denominations state this paragraph in different ways. However, keep your comments brief. You just finished preaching a stewardship sermon.]

By this time, the ushers have completed their distribution of the *Estimate of Giving Cards*. Remove a card from your pocket, and say, "Please read along with me on the *Estimate of Giving Card*."

- Read the card aloud, word for word. After reading the first box that says "Step Up Beyond Tithing," say, "If you are already beyond tithing and you intend to increase your giving more, check this first box."
- Then read the next two box statements.
- Emphasize the box that tells whether this is an increase from last year. Say, "If this is true of what you will be writing on your card, please check the box. This is extremely helpful to the financial secretary when she (or he) tabulates the results for announcement at the end of our Celebration Luncheon in a few minutes."
- Say, "Also, would you please help us by printing your full address in the blanks?"

"After we pray together, please take whatever time you need to meditate and complete your card. When you have done that, please move quietly to the front of the church, since others are still working on their cards. Place your card here on the table as a worshipful act of dedication.

"We ordinarily conclude our worship service with a benediction. The final *Amen* at the end of a benediction means 'so be it.' Today we close our service with each worshipper saying a final 'amen—so let it be' by placing his or her card on the table as an act of consecration.

"After you place your card on the table, please leave the sanctuary silently on your way to the Celebration Luncheon so as not to disturb the meditation of others who are still completing their cards."

The guest leader prays a brief prayer of dedication and leaves silently by a side aisle. She or he should also include a table grace so that members won't feel awkward beginning to eat.

Step #10: After leaving the sanctuary, go directly to the church office where the financial secretary and assistant are ready to begin working on the tabulations for the report. Answer any questions they may have about that process.

Guest Leader Guide | 107

Make certain that they have all the information for the report blanks that must be prepared ahead of time, such as the total dollars given for the last twelve months, the three-year average of loose offerings, and information to calculate the coming year's giving total for regular givers who are not present today.

Be prepared for that 1 percent to 5 percent of instances in which a negative-thinking or confused financial secretary seems determined to sabotage the program by not providing the figure for one or more of these blanks. If that happens, be firm. Insist, "We cannot give the report without filling in all the blanks. Would you get those figures, or we'll have to say we don't have all the information we need to make the final report?"

Encourage (or confront) recalcitrant financial types with, "Members are not likely to stop being Christians at the end of this giving year. Last year's totals from regular givers not present today are far more reliable in some way than the new estimates of giving. Those regular givers already have proven that they are dependable donors and will give at least the amount they already are giving."

> **The Bottom Line:** If you faithfully followed all ten steps and motivated the Consecration Sunday team to accomplish the timeline tasks to the letter, having a program end with other than positive results is virtually impossible. Everyone wins. The team wins! You win! The church wins! God wins! Congratulations!

NOTES

NOTES

NOTES

NOTES

www.ingramcontent.com/pod-product-compliance
Lightning Source LLC
Chambersburg PA
CBHW080808300426
44114CB00020B/2867